GOING AROUND IN
ACADEMIC CIRCLES

GOING AROUND

WITH ILLUSTRATIONS BY LEO HERSHFIELD

McGraw-Hill Book Company
New York · Toronto · London

Richard Armour

IN ACADEMIC CIRCLES

A LOW VIEW OF HIGHER EDUCATION

GOING AROUND IN ACADEMIC CIRCLES

Library of Congress Catalog Card Number:
65-22953
First Edition
02234

Dedicated to

SOCRATES

the first professor to drink himself to death

ACKNOWLEDGMENTS

My thanks go to all concerned for permission to include the following pieces, previously published: "A Short History of Higher Education," Editorial Projects for Education, Inc.; "Professor Emeritus," *The Georgia Review;* "Dean of the Faculty," "Faculty Meeting," "Professor's Progress," "Academic Procession," and "Twenty-Fifth Reunion," *The Pacific Spectator;* "Eight O'Clock Class," *College English;* "Librarian," *The Saturday Evening Post;* "Young Instructor," *Claremont Quarterly;* "How to Burn a Book," *California Librarian.*

CONTENTS

I

PRE-REGISTRATION

One day, when my son was a junior in high school, he came to me for a man-to-man talk. I knew it was to be a man-to-man talk, because we had had the last boy-to-man talk the year before, about girls, and he had drawn even. In fact he had got a little ahead.

"Dad," he said, "my counselor thinks I should start planning for college."

This came as no surprise to me. I had been saving for my son's college education for five years, and now had enough to see him through the first semester.

"Your counselor is right," I said. "And what sort of planning does he have in mind?"

"Well," my son said, "like what college to go to."

"Does he have any suggestions?"

"He thinks I ought to go to a small college, maybe in the Middle West."

"What," I asked, "makes him think so?"

"Well, he says at a small college you don't get lost."

"Couldn't you go to a large university and carry a compass?"

"Come off it, Dad. He means that at a small college you're an individual. At a big university you're just a number."

"Maybe he's got a university mixed up with a penitentiary."

"Can't you be serious for a minute? This is one of the biggest decisions of my life. My counselor said so."

"Oh, all right," I said. "By the way, what kind of college did your counselor go to?"

"Well, to a small college."

"And in what part of the country?"

"In the Middle West."

"I thought so," I said.

"You mean you think he's prejudiced?"

"Loyal might be a better word for it. It might be interesting to find out what a Yale man would say, or a graduate of Tulane or Stanford."

"But you don't know my counselor. He knows about *all* the colleges. He knows *everything* about colleges."

I didn't wait for my son to tell me his counselor knew *everything* about *everything*. I turned on my heel (which up to then had been turned off) and walked out. I realize now, as I realized then, that I was jealous. Why hadn't my son come straight to me, if he wanted to know what college to go to? Do you think I went to a counselor, when I started thinking about college? Of course not. I had too much respect for my father, and besides, there was no such thing as a counselor in those days.

"Father," I said to my father.

"What?" he said, coming directly to the point.

"I wonder whether I can go to college."

"I think we can manage it, if you earn your way."

"Thank you, father," I said. "I'll try to be worth every penny I spend on myself."

"Have you thought of where you might go?"

"No, sir, I was leaving that to you."

"Why not go to the college right here in town? It would save train fare."

And the local college was the one I went to. My father had gone there also. But unlike the counselor who counseled my son, he wasn't loyal. He was practical.

In sharp contrast with my son, when the time came for my daughter to select a college, she came directly to me and asked my opinion. I made a careful study of catalogues, talked with graduates, deans of admission, and other parents, and came up with a list of several institutions, any one of which seemed to me suitable. She was very grateful.

"Thank you, Dad," she said, "for going to all that work."

Shortly afterward she chose a college not on my list, because a friend was going there.

I may not know *everything* about colleges, like that counselor. But after attending a small college in the West and a large graduate school in the East, and after teaching at seven colleges and universities in various parts of the country, I know a *few* things about the academic world. This inside story comes too late to help my son and daughter, but it may be useful to other young people. As for my colleagues in the teaching profession—if this is familiar material, they will at least have the pleasure of recognition. My only hope is that they will not recognize themselves. If they do, it is because all academic people look a little alike and, alas, act a little alike. They may think they recognize themselves, when it is only someone who looks and acts like them. It is an understandable mistake.

Having mentioned my teaching at seven colleges and universities, I should add that I left each of these institutions voluntarily, in search of greater happiness and higher pay (which, to a college professor, are synonymous). I was a peripatetic, wandering about like the great teachers of ancient Greece, followed by their followers. But in all honesty I must say that I know of not a single (or married) student who left, for example, the University of Texas to follow me to Northwestern University. And I am glad, because I moved from place to place in search not only of better pay but of better students.

Now we are ready to ask an Academic Question, which is a safe kind of question to ask, because it is utterly unlikely to produce any practical result. The question is: What is college really like?

But first let us see how higher education began, how

An academic question

it progressed, becoming progressively more progressive, what its *raison d'être* is (the first foreign phrase used so far, which shows admirable restraint, since I know several others), and whether there is any future for it. This means going back to the Stone Age, which some academic people refer to fondly as the Good Old Days, before departmental rivalry, emphasis on publication, questionnaires, and picketing by students.

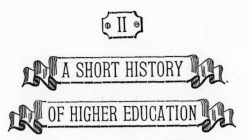

II

A SHORT HISTORY
OF HIGHER EDUCATION

Prehistoric Times

Little is known about higher education during the Stone Age, which is perhaps just as well.

Because of a weakness in the liberal arts, the B.A. was not offered, and there was only the B.S., or Bachelor of Stones. Laboratory facilities were meager, owing to lack of government contracts and support from private industry, but the stars were readily available on clear nights for those interested in astronomy.

Prehistoric students, being before history, failed to comprehend the fundamentals of the subject, such as its being divided into Ancient, Medieval, and Modern.

There were no college boards.

Nor were there any fraternities. The only clubs on the campus were those carried by the students.

Alumni organizations were in their infancy, where some of them have remained. The Alumni Secretary occupied a small cave, left behind when the Director of Development moved to a larger one. While waiting for contributions to come in, he idly doodled on the

The only clubs on campus

wall, completely unaware that art critics would some-day mistake his drawings of certain members of the board of trustees for dinosaurs and saber-toothed tigers.

The Alumni Quarterly came out every quarter of a century, and was as eagerly awaited as it is today.

The Classical Period

In ancient Athens everyone knew Greek, and in ancient Rome everyone knew Latin, even small children—

which those who have taken Elementary Greek or Elementary Latin will find hard to believe. Universities wishing to teach a language which had little practical use but was good for mental discipline could have offered English if they had thought of it.

Buildings were all in the classical style, and what looked like genuine marble was genuine marble.

The professors of the Peripatetic School kept moving

The little Greek schoolhouse

from town to town, closely followed by students and creditors. Sometimes lectures were held in the Groves of Academe, where students could munch apples and occasionally cast an anxious eye at birds in the branches overhead.

Under the Caesars, taxation became so burdensome that Romans in the upper brackets found they might as well give money to their Alma Mater instead of letting the State have it. Thus it was that crowds often gathered along the Appian Way to applaud a spirited chariot race between the chairman of the funds drive and the tax collector, each trying to get to a good prospect first.

The word "donor" comes from the Latin *donare*, to give, and is not to be confused with *dunare*, to dun, though it frequently is.

When a prominent alumnus was thrown to the lions, customary procedure in the alumni office was to observe a moment of silence. Then the secretary, wrapping his toga a little more tightly around him, solemnly declared, "Well, we might as well take him off the cultivation list."

The Middle Ages

In the period known as the Dark Ages, or nighthood, higher education survived only because of illuminated manuscripts, which were discovered during a routine burning of a library. It is interesting to reconstruct a typical classroom scene: a group of dedicated students clustered around a glowing piece of parchment, listening to a lecture in Advanced Monasticism, a ten-year course. If some found it hard to concentrate, it was because they were dreaming about quitting before exams and going off on a crusade.

Some left even sooner, before the end of the lecture, having spied a beautiful damsel being pursued by a dragon who had designs on her. The dragon was probably an art student who was out of drawing paper. Damsels, who were invariably in distress, wrought havoc on a young man's grade-point average.

Asking for a promotion

Members of the faculty were better off than previously, because they wore suits of armor. Fully accoutered, and with their visors down, they could summon up enough courage to go into the President's office and ask for a promotion even though they had not published a thing.

At this time the alumni council became more aggressive in its fund drives, using such persuasive devices as the thumbscrew, the knout, the rack, and the wheel. A wealthy alumnus would usually donate generously if a sufficient number of alumni could cross his moat and storm his castle walls. A few could be counted on to survive the rain of stones, arrows, and molten lead. Such a group of alumni, known as "the committee," was customarily conducted to the castle by a troubadour, who led in the singing of the Alma Mater Song the while.

The Renaissance

During the Renaissance, universities sprang up all over Europe. You could go to bed at night, with not a university around, and the next morning there would be two universities right down the street, each with a faculty, student body, campanile, and need for additional endowment.

The first universities were in Italy, where Dante was required reading. Boccaccio was not required but was read anyhow, and in the original Italian, so much being lost in translation. Other institutions soon followed, such as Heidelberg, where a popular elective was Duelling 103a, b, usually taken concurrently with Elementary First Aid. In England there was Oxford, where, by curious coincidence, all of the young instructors were named Don. There was also Cambridge.

The important thing about the Renaissance, which was a time of awakening (even in the classroom), was education of the Whole Man. Previously such vital parts as the elbows and ear lobes had been neglected. The graduate of a university was supposed, above all, to be a Gentleman. This meant that he should know such things as archery, falconry, and fencing (subjects now largely relegated to Physical Education and given only one-half credit per semester), as well as, in the senior year, how to use a knife and fork.

During the Renaissance, the works of Homer, Virgil, and other classical writers were rediscovered, much to the annoyance of students.

Alumni officials concentrated their efforts on securing a patron: someone rich like Lorenzo de' Medici, some-one clever like Machiavelli, or (if they wished to get rid of a troublesome member of the administration) someone really useful like Lucrezia Borgia.

Colonial America

The first universities in America were founded by the Puritans. This explains the strict regulations about Late Hours, Compulsory Chapel, and No Liquor on the Campus which still exist at many institutions.

Some crafts were taught, but witchcraft was an extra-curricular activity. Witch-burning, on the other hand, was the seventeenth-century equivalent of hanging a football coach in effigy at the end of a bad season.

Though deplored, it was passed off by the authorities as attributable to "youthful exuberance."

Harvard set the example for naming colleges after donors. William and Mary, though making a good try, failed to start a trend for using first names. It was more successful, however, in starting Phi Beta Kappa, a fraternity which permitted no rough stuff in its initiations. At first the Phi Beta Kappa key was worn on the key ring, but the practice went out with the discovery of the watch chain and vest.

During the Colonial Period, alumni officials limited their fund-raising activities to alumni who were securely fastened, hands and legs, in the stocks. In this position they were completely helpless and gave generously, or could be frisked.

Revolutionary America

Higher education came to a virtual standstill during the Revolution—every able-bodied male having enlisted for the duration. Since the ROTC had not yet been established, college men were forced to have other qualifications for a commission, such as money.

General George Washington was given an honorary degree by Harvard, and this helped see him through the difficult winter at Valley Forge. Since he gave no commencement address, it is assumed that he made a substantial contribution to the building fund. Then again, mindful of the reputation he had gained through

Parson Weems's cherry tree story, he may have established a chair in Ethics.

Unlike the situation during World War I, when colleges and universities abandoned the teaching of German in order to humiliate the Kaiser, the Colonists waged the Revolutionary War successfully without prohibiting the teaching of English. They did, however, force students to substitute such good old American words as "suspenders" for "braces," and themes were marked down when the spelling "tyre" was used for "tire."

The alumni publication, variously called the Alumni Bulletin, the Alumni Quarterly, and the Alumni Newsletter, was probably invented at this time by Benjamin Franklin, who invented almost everything else, including bifocals and kites. The first such publication was *Poor Alumnus' Almanac*, full of such homely sayings as "Early to bed and early to rise makes a man healthy, wealthy, and wise enough to write his Alma Mater into his will."

Contemporary America

In the nineteenth century, denominational colleges were founded in all parts of the country, especially Ohio. In the smaller of these colleges, money was mostly given in small denominations. A few colleges were not named after John Wesley.

State universities came into being at about the same

time, and were tax supported. Every taxpayer was therefore a donor, but without getting his name on a building or being invited to dinner by the President. The taxpayer, in short, was in the same class as the Anonymous Giver, but not because he asked that his name be withheld. It was some of his salary that was withheld.

About the middle of the nineteenth century, women were admitted to college. This was done (1) to relieve men of having to take women's parts in dramatic productions, some women's parts being hard for men to supply, (2) to provide cheer leaders with shapelier legs and therefore more to cheer about, and (3) to recruit members for the Women's Glee Club. It was not realized, when they were admitted, that women would get most of the high marks, especially from professors who graded on curves.

In the twentieth century, important strides were made, such as the distinction which developed between education and Education. Teachers came to be trained in what were at first called Normal Schools. With the detection of certain abnormalities, the name was changed to Teachers Colleges.

John Dewey introduced Progressive Education, whereby students quickly knew more than their teachers and told them so. Robert Hutchins turned the University of Chicago upside down, thereby necessitating a new building program. At St. John's College everyone studied the Great Books, which were more economical because they did not come out each year in a revised edition. Educational television gave college professors an excuse for owning a television set, which they had previously maintained would destroy the reading habit. This made it possible for them to watch Westerns and old movies without losing status.

Of recent years, an increasing number of students spend their junior year abroad. This enables them to get a glimpse of professors who are away on Fulbrights or Guggenheims.

Student government has grown apace, students now not only governing themselves but giving valuable suggestions, in the form of ultimatums, to the President and Dean. In wide use is the Honor System, which makes the professor leave the room during an examination because he is not to be trusted.

Along with these improvements in education has come a subtle change in the American alumnus. No longer interested only in the record of his college's football team, he is likely to appear at his class reunion full of such penetrating questions as "Why is the tuition higher than it was in 1934?" "Is it true that 85 per cent of the faculty are Communists?" and "How can I get my son (or daughter) in?"

Alumni magazines have kept pace with such advances. The writing has improved, thanks to schools of journalism, until there is excitement and suspense even

A penetrating question

in the obituary column. Expression has reached such a high point of originality that a request for funds may appear, at first reading, to be a gift offer.

All in all, higher education has reached these heights of attainment:

Despite their questionable contribution to earning a living, the liberal arts are accepted as an excellent means of keeping young people off the streets for four years.

Young people, in turn, are continuing their studies longer and longer, having discovered this an excellent means of keeping out of the Army.

Faculty members, publishing more voluminously than ever, are making an important contribution to the national economy, especially to the pulp and paper industry.

The government is helping students with scholarships and professors with research grants, thereby enabling more and more students to go to college, where more and more professors are too busy with research grants to teach them.

Having surveyed the history of higher education from the Stone Age to the present, let us now make a careful analysis, or Study in Depth, of college today.

III

THE CATALOGUE

The first thing a prospective student should do is to send for a catalogue (also known as a catalog). Since it is important to make a good impression, the form of the letter should be correct. A specimen letter is as follows:

Dear Sir:
    Please send me a copy of your catalogue.
        Sincerely yours,

After the letter is sent, days of happy anticipation follow. Watching the mailbox can be fun and also rewarding, because while watching the mailbox the watcher may see all sorts of other things, some of them fairly interesting. For instance one mailbox watcher saw a white-breasted nuthatch. Another saw a pair of Blackburnian warblers.

At last the catalogue arrives. What excitement! What cries of "The catalogue! The catalogue!" and "Mommy,

Watching the mailbox

it's here!" Trembling fingers have difficulty opening the large manila envelope, on which are the telltale words, "Educational Materials." Just think of it, *Educational!*

The envelope is opened and the catalogue is removed. It is not a large volume—nine inches long, five inches wide, and perhaps half an inch thick. But one is mindful, if one owns a copy of Bartlett's *Familiar Quotations*, of Marlowe's famous line, "Infinite riches in a little room." For the catalogue is full of pearls of great price, produced by academic oysters.

Since the catalogue has no author as such, it is difficult to fix the responsibility for omissions, misstatements, and typographical errors. Among those involved in the preparation of the catalogue are the Dean of the Faculty, the Dean of Admissions, the Director of Public

Information, the Chairman of the Faculty Committee on Publications, and an office secretary who does the entire job: collects material, rewrites whatever is wordy or unclear, makes arrangements with the printer, and reads proof.

The President, too, plays an important part in the preparation of the catalogue. From time to time he asks searching questions of the Dean of the Faculty, Dean of Admissions, Director of Public Information, and Chairman of the Faculty Committee on Publications. One of these questions is: "When will the catalogue be out?" Another is: "What the devil is holding up the catalogue?" When the President receives the first copy of the new catalogue, he examines it carefully, wishing to make sure his latest honorary degree has been included.

Though the catalogue is published in a larger first printing than most novels, it is not customarily sent to review media. This is fortunate, because it would be difficult if not impossible to classify it either as fiction or nonfiction, as an adult book or a juvenile, though it is obviously an original paperback. The reviewer would also be handicapped by the lack of a publisher's summary on the jacket flap. If, however, the catalogue were to fall into the hands of, say, a critic writing for *The Kenyon Review*, we might anticipate something of this sort:

Not in many years has such an original work come to our attention. *Catalogue* is refreshing in its approach to the human predicament, straightforward in expression but with mystic, almost poetic overtones. The setting of this story is an idyllic spot where the climate is equable and every pleasure imaginable is within easy reach. A friendly atmosphere prevails. Though there are certain regulations and requirements, wisely prescribed to keep the community from degenerating into meaningless hedonism, the emphasis is on pleasurable mental and physical activity.

Catalogue is obviously in the tradition of utopian writings which began, at least in our Greco-Roman culture, with Plato's *Republic*, and continued with Sir Thomas More's *Utopia* and similar writings. As in such works, there is an element of satire or reproof in the contrast between life within this ideal community, where philosophic calm prevails, and life outside its walls, infected by the febrile madness of materialistic competition.

But what gives *Catalogue* its special quality is a hint of something beyond the palpable and pragmatic. This is inherent in the frequently repeated phrase, "preparation for life." While other interpretations are possible, this would seem to suggest that persons living in this fanciful elysium, comparable to that envisaged in the last act of Shelley's *Prometheus Unbound*, exist or pre-exist in some form of limbo, purgatory, or pre-natal state. They have not yet "lived," at least in the sense commonly understood. References to "Commencement" give further credence to this theory, since "life," or life as we know it, begins only after completion of some

Commencement, when life begins

kind of mental and physical gestation, lasting for a period, usually, of four years.

Two groups of people mingle in what is referred to ambiguously as "a close personal relationship." These two groups or strata, living in a rather rigid but generally accepted caste system, are known as Professors and Students. The two groups dwell apart in a segregated society, though Students apparently from time to time visit Professors for what is euphemistically called "social intercourse" or, sometimes, "stimulation."

One technique borrowed from the drama is the listing of the principal characters or cast (see the reference to caste above) at the beginning of the book. Otherwise the form is more like that of a novel, or novella, in which the forward movement of the plot is broken by the interposition of episodic elements. One such interpolated element, "Calendar for the Academic Year," appears to be intended as a reminder of mortality or of the *Ars longa, vita brevis* of Hippocrates.

In the main, however, the form is picaresque, after the manner of Cervantes or Defoe, in which a single protagonist, The Student, is followed from entrance into the utopian community to "graduation" (see the *Gradus ad Parnassum* of the early schoolmen in England) into a life for which he is either conditioned by his experiences or from which he has mercifully been spared during the above-mentioned quadrennium. An even better parallel than the picaresque works of Cervantes and Defoe, since The Student is not delineated as a *pícaro*, or rogue, might be Bunyan's *Pilgrim's Progress*. Indeed the resemblance of The Student to Bunyan's central character, Christian, is striking. There is an ingenious reversal in *Catalogue*, however, for the pilgrimage of The Student is not through life to Heaven but through Heaven to life.

This is not a book which will have popular appeal, since many readers will miss its subtleties and nuances. However, the reader who is knowledgeable in history, religion, philosophy, art, literature, and the sciences, all of which are woven into this erudite but imaginative work, and who is conversant with Hegel, Schopenhauer, Sartre, Kafka, and some of the other great names mentioned with offhand casualness will find *Catalogue* an unusual and rewarding book.

At most colleges, even those which are church-supported, the catalogue is the Bible. Everyone keeps a copy close at hand for reference, and many, especially members of the faculty and administration, can quote favorite passages which give them solace and inspiration in times of need. Passages subject to various interpretations are referred to the Academic Council, which hands down rulings much as the Supreme Court does on the Constitution. Changes in wording, such as substitution of "the" for "a" in a crucial passage, may be recommended by the Dean but require approval by a two-thirds vote of the faculty.

The catalogue is, in short, an Important Document. Though England has got along for centuries with an unwritten constitution, it is hard to imagine a college getting through even a day with an unwritten catalogue.

Once, in fact, a professor's life was saved by a catalogue. The professor was shot by an enraged student, who got a D when he thought he should have had a C, and the catalogue, in the professor's breast pocket, deflected the bullet. This shows how important it is always to have a catalogue on one's person, and why students should check for catalogue-size bulges in the region of a professor's heart before wasting ammunition.

IV

HOW TO GET IN

Let us assume that the prospective student has read the catalogue and, naively accepting all of its statements as true, has decided, "This is the college for me." Let us also assume, though it is usually my practice to be quite unassuming, that the prospective student has filled out all the blanks and paid the necessary deposit. What then?

A curious thing about college admissions is that while students are trying to get in, colleges are trying to get students. The reason for this is that the colleges the students are trying to get into and the students the colleges are trying to get often don't match.

"I'd give everything I have," says Bert Smathers, "to get into Harvard."

But what does young Smathers have? An average of not quite C during his last two years at Central High, a CEEB verbal score of 367, no athletic ability, and a personality that won him his only award in high school, that of being voted Creep of the Year. Moreover, having no financial resources, he will need a scholarship sufficient to cover at least such essentials as room, board, and tuition.

"I think I'll go to a state university in the Middle West," says H. Saltonstall Lowell. "I detest the snobbishness and provincialism of places like Harvard."

Young Lowell graduated first in his class at Choate, racked up a CEEB verbal score of 800 and a math score of 790, captained the undefeated tennis team, set track records for the 100 and 220, and was president of the student body. Since his father, a member of the Harvard Board of Overseers, is a major stockholder in General Pneumatics, he would not require financial assistance.

As a Dean of Admissions said, when told of the above cases, "That's the way the cooky crumbles." He appeared fatalistic, even nonchalant, but he was unable to control the tear that rolled down his cheek.

To find and persuade students like H. Saltonstall Lowell, most colleges have a Field Representative, constantly prowling the countryside. Seen on a train or airplane, he could not be distinguished from an insurance salesman or a manufacturer's representative, except for his constantly humming the Alma Mater. At the schools he visits, appointments are set up with any students interested in the college he represents, and since this means a great deal to some students, such as getting out of class, he usually has a full day of interviews.

When the Field Representative has tracked down a student who would be a real catch, one who would make both Phi Beta Kappa and the All-Conference football team, the interview goes something like this:

Student: What's so special about your college?

Field Representative: Well, for one thing, many of the classes are very small. (He doesn't say why they are small. They are small because the professors who teach them are either dull or uninformed. In the extremely small classes they may be both. Nor does he explain the disadvantages of a small class, such as being missed if you are absent.)

Student: What about faculty-student relationships outside of class?

Field Representative: They are close. (This means it is always possible to make an appointment with a professor, and sometimes he will remember to keep it.)

Student: How is the food?

Field Representative: Marvelous. (The Field Representative looks well fed, and no wonder, since he never eats at the college.)

Student: Is liquor allowed on the campus?

Field Representative (Who looks horrified, either because (1) of course it isn't or (2) of course it is. In either case it is a stupid question, and the Field Representative pretends not to have heard it): Well, I think it's time for the next appointment. It's been great talking with you.

Student: Don't I get any samples or anything?

Field Representative: Of course. (He gives him a pennant, copies of several publications, including last year's commencement address, "The Liberal Arts in Transition, and a memorial ash tray, embellished with the college motto, the famous admonition of Publius Ibid, *"Vide supra et vide infra."*)

The Field Representative submits a confidential report to the Dean of Admissions. This report can be very helpful in evaluating an applicant, since it is full of such perceptive remarks as: "Wouldn't fit into our student body. Too intellectual." Or "Weak student and poor citizen, but father owns local brewery and might help with our new chapel." Once a Field Representative, an attractive young man who had graduated only a couple of years before, made the following report on an exceptional find: "This girl has everything—brains, beauty, talent. But she has decided not to go to college. We are getting married."

Now a few pointers for applicants who wish to know on what basis they are likely to be judged. Of course high school grades are important, especially in such solids as English, history, Latin, and chemistry. Grades in liquids such as domestic science (to be distinguished from imported science), music appreciation, and basket weaving fail to impress the authorities unless they are unusually low, say a B. The school, too, makes a difference, some schools having an even poorer reputation than others. Also it means more to be in the first ten in a graduating class of six hundred than in a graduating class of six.

As for College Board scores, these are so mechanical and depend so much on how the student feels on the day of the test that they carry little weight with anyone but admissions officials.

"What chance is there for my son, who made terribly low scores on both the Verbal and Mathematical tests?" a parent is likely to ask, somewhat discouraged.

"Every chance in the world," the Dean of Admissions says reassuringly. "He's probably just a slow maturer."

"What do you advise?"

A slow maturer

"Wait until he matures," the Dean of Admissions says helpfully.

By waiting a few years, the applicant may become mature enough to realize how unnecessary a college education is, by that time being the head of his firm.

It might interest parents and prospective students to know that the Dean of Admissions is assisted by a faculty committee which has no confidence whatsoever in the judgment of the Dean of Admissions.

"He hasn't a Ph.D.," one member of the committee says, his upper lip curling derisively.

"And he hasn't published a line, not so much as a book review," says another.

"He's not even a member of Phi Beta Kappa, just some Education fraternity," adds a third, making a thumbs-down motion with one hand while twirling his Phi Beta Kappa key with the other.

If it were not for the members of the faculty committee, someone who is not a "brain" but has character, drive, originality, and high qualities of leadership might slip in and become president of the student body. The faculty is concerned about academic excellence, hoping to admit so many students of intellectual brilliance that a fair percentage will go on to win Fulbrights and Woodrow Wilsons, no matter how poorly they are taught.

Students are advised to apply to several colleges, not merely the college of their choice. This is because each application must be accompanied by a fee, which is non-returnable, and every little bit helps when the budget is tight. Students who are afraid they will not get into any college are advised to submit their names to a central organization which keeps a list of colleges which are not well known, because they are unable to afford a football coach, or even a football. Then again, their moral standards may be so high that they have failed to gain national attention through headlines such as STUDENT CUT BY BUSTED BOTTLE DURING BEER BUST or COLLEGE PREXY ADMITS KEEPING DEAN OF WOMEN IN LOVE NEST. But students can learn a great deal at such colleges, even when they are church-connected, if there is a large city nearby.

Outstanding students are given Honors at Entrance. If they continue to do well for four years, they are given Honors at Exit.

Inquiries should be addressed to the Dean of Admissions, who hopes there will not be too many, at least until the new secretary, the third this year, learns to type.

V

THE CAMPUS

The first thing a new student is likely to see is the college gates, on which will be found an inspiring inscription, such as "Beat Tech," written in black with large, free brush strokes. Under this inscription can be faintly seen another, carved in the stone, which is in Latin and more wordy and less memorable. Near the gates is a stone bench on which someone is sitting who is waiting for someone who is sitting on the stone bench near the gates on the other side of the campus.

The student arrives either alone and thoroughly frightened or with his parents and thoroughly embarrassed.

"I don't mind your going to the business office to pay my bills," says the student who is accompanied by his parents, "but then I think you'd better go on home."

"But I want to fix up your room nice and comfy," his mother says, unpacking the draperies with the flowered pattern.

"And I'd like to meet your faculty adviser and talk over your program," says his father. "I also want to see whether he's a pinko."

Inspiring inscription

Daughters are less embarrassed by parents than sons, but surveys reveal that students are overwhelmingly of the same opinion: to wit, that parents should stay home, writing letters and enclosing checks.

Just inside the gates is a walk which runs across the campus. You would think a walk would walk across the campus, but it doesn't. Apparently it is in a hurry to get where it is going, like everybody else. If college is in session, students may be seen on the walks, hurrying to class. If they are not hurrying, it means that they are already so late it makes no difference.

When two boys are walking together, one is likely to be reading something. What he is reading is notes that will help him pass the examination he is going to take in a few minutes. The reason he is walking with the other boy is that these are the other boy's notes.

When two girls are walking together, neither one is likely to be reading anything. This is because they are Prepared. Being Prepared is one reason a professor likes to have girls in his classes, especially girls who sit on the front row and have nice legs.

On either side of the walk are hedges. These are meant to keep students from walking on the grass but have no effect whatsoever. It is always possible to jump over a low hedge or to find a thin spot in a high hedge and make it thinner by going through it every day. Some students, however, do not walk on the grass. They sit on it and lie on it. On any pleasant spring day you can find a student lying on the grass with a book in his hand, sound asleep. Members of the Grounds Force are too respectful of students to tell them to get off the grass. The only thing they can do is turn on the sprinklers. If it weren't for students who lie on the grass, the grass would not be so pretty and green from so much sprinkling.

The campus is covered with beautiful trees of many varieties, chiefly those which drop their leaves one at a time and keep the campus looking untidy. Everyone knows Joyce Kilmer's lines about trees, which is one of several good reasons for not quoting them here.

This brings us to the buildings which rise spectacularly from the campus. One which does not rise very spectacularly is the Home Economics building, which is only one story. It is wooden, in need of a paint job, and has several times been declared a Fire Hazard. However, there is a fire extinguisher just inside the front door, and if it works, the building can be saved, unfortunately.

A landmark on the campus is Old Main. This building is exceptional not only because it was one of the original buildings of the college but because it is the only building not named after anyone. Unless, that is, it was named after an elderly donor named Main.

Anyhow, Old Main is a landmark, which means that you can see it from almost any direction despite all the trees and vines that it was hoped would eventually hide it. Old Main is a red brick building in a style of architecture so distinctive that it has come to be known as Old Main Style, or 19th Century Hideous. It has steps in front which are used for rallies, but its most noticeable feature is its bell tower. One of the distinctive things about the bell tower is that it has no bell. There was originally a bell, but it was removed during the Spanish-American War to be made into cannon balls. After the war, they never got around to making the cannon balls back into a bell. Now the bell tower is chiefly used as a place to hang people in effigy—people like the Head Coach and the President, with their name on a sign in front in case you don't recognize them.

Old Main has the squeakiest floors of any building on the campus. It isn't necessary to knock on the door of an office in Old Main. The people in the office know visitors are coming and how close they are getting. Mostly the rooms are occupied by the Administration and by the English Department. The English Department is happy to be under a roof anywhere. It moved into Old Main when a new building was built for the Social Studies Department, which had changed its name to the Behavioral Sciences and tripled in size.

As a matter of fact, the English Department is glad to have anything that is not needed by one of the more important departments. It has always been grateful for the pencil sharpener which was no longer needed by Physics, when Physics stopped using pencils on account of the machine that now does all its writing and most of its thinking. As soon as Chemistry perfects its condensed water pill, the English Department hopes to get Chemistry's drinking fountain and not have to go all the way to the basement of the Library rather than take a chance of getting caught drinking with the President or the Dean of the Faculty.

The Library and the Science Building are the newest on the campus and are in the same style of architecture, which is true of no other two buildings. Some think this gives the campus a sort of sameness. The style of architecture is Modern, which means there is so much glass that you can tell who is there without going inside. There are also a great many straight lines, and since a straight line is the shortest distance between two points, this should have been economical. Actually they are the most expensive buildings on the campus, because they were built by an architect and a contractor who are on the Board of Trustees.

The Library and the Science Building are the only buildings which are air-conditioned, the Library to keep books in good condition and the Science Building to keep members of the science faculty from going into industry.

Dormitories and other facilities will be discussed in a subsequent chapter. But a word should be said at this point concerning the Master Plan. This is a plan for buying several acres of adjoining land from individuals who, knowing the college has to expand, refuse to sell until they get "their price," which is five times what they paid for it. The Master Plan also envisages tearing down all the old college buildings and putting up new buildings with air conditioning, piped-in music, and educational TV. Drawings of the Master Plan fill one wall of the President's office and are shown to any visitor who is rich, old, in poor health, and without heirs.

When such a person is brought into the President's office, preferably in a wheel chair, by the Director of Development, a conversation like this ensues:

"How *do* you do?" asks the President, who really wants to know. As he shakes hands with his visitor, he fumbles a bit, trying at the same time to feel his pulse.

Prospective donor

"Tolerable," says the visitor, a man of many dollars and few words.

"Please sit over here," says the President, deftly arranging for the old fellow to face the Master Plan. "I'm *so* happy to see you."

"Don't know that I can say the same," says the visitor, who can afford anything, including being rude.

"That's a good one," says the President, laughing uproariously. "You have a wonderful sense of humor."

"Give it to me straight, Prexy. How much do you want?"

Picking up a pointer, the President points hopefully to a small rectangle on the Master Plan. "The new Music Building is something we need desperately," he says. "The architect says it could be built for $300,000." He knows perfectly well that the architect habitually underestimates a trifle, and it will cost all of $800,000, plus $600,000 endowment for upkeep. But he figures if he gets the building started, others will help out rather than see the thing left without some of the refinements, such as a roof.

"Cheap enough," says the visitor, now become a Benefactor. "I'll see my broker tomorrow and turn over $300,000 worth of AT&T and Standard Oil of New Jersey. That'll save me having to pay the capital gains tax."

"Fine," says the President. "Anything to do the government out of a little money, eh?" He winks confidentially at the Benefactor, who winks back, and they both have a hearty laugh at the expense of the Bureau of Internal Revenue.

The Master Plan is $300,000 closer realization.

Or it would have been, if the Benefactor hadn't fallen that night and broken his hip. Two weeks later he died of Complications, without ever having transferred the stock to the college. When his will was probated, it was found that he left every penny to his mistress, a retired operatic contralto.

Had the college known about her? Of course. Why else would the President have used the Music Building ploy?

"We want to keep after donors who haven't long to live," said the President, as he and his Director of Development sat staring gloomily at the architect's rendering of the Master Plan. "But for God's sake, don't cut it too close!"

VI

RESIDENCE AND RECREATIONAL FACILITIES

Dormitories are an important feature of the campus, because without them students would have to live in motels or rooming houses or at home or somewhere equally undesirable. There are two kinds of dormitories: Men's and Women's. Men's dormitories are full of windows that can be climbed out of, and women's dormitories are full of windows that can be climbed into. Students usually refer to a dormitory as a "dorm," thus saving three syllables. This abbreviation can cause misunderstanding, however. For instance there was the time a wealthy donor said to the President, "I don't give a dorm." The President thought the man was cussing, but it turned out that he wanted to give a gymnasium, not a dormitory.

Dormitories have a homelike atmosphere, especially for students who come from homes with a couple of hundred bedrooms, each of them occupied by a stranger who moves in for a stay of nine months and, as soon as he gets in, turns on his radio. It is amazing how soon a brand-new dormitory can have that friendly, lived-in look, with cigarette burns on the tables and numbers all over the wall next to the telephone.

A welcome feature of dormitories is the parlor, in which students of the opposite sex and faculty guests can be entertained. It usually takes several students to entertain a faculty guest, but one student can entertain one student of the opposite sex quite satisfactorily. If the parlor becomes too crowded, some students will considerately excuse themselves and, giving up the comfort of the parlor, continue to entertain as best they can in a parked car.

Many of the dormitory rooms are singles, but there are also doubles which give the student the opportunity of enjoying the company of a roommate. Roommates are chosen by a secretary in the office of the Dean of Admissions who has a special talent for matching persons no one else would ever think of putting together. Part of the secret of her success is the questionnaire sent out to each incoming student. The questionnaire asks such questions as:

Do you smoke?

If you smoke, do you make a habit of blowing the smoke into the faces of non-smokers?

Are you an early riser, and do you do calisthenics to music immediately upon rising?

Are you a liberal or a conservative politically?

Do you sometimes come to blows with those who disagree with you?

Once all the completed questionnaires have been received, the secretary carefully arranges them alphabetically and then drops them into a wastebasket. She does not wish to be prejudiced by facts.

This same system was in effect when I was in college, and my roommate was responsible for one of the most traumatic experiences of my life. I was a quiet, shy, unathletic introvert. My roommate was a loud, muscular fellow, a second-string halfback. While I studied, he liked to call signals, "Fifty-three, twenty-six, eighty-four, HUP!" and throw himself a pass. This he did by bouncing the ball off the wall over my head, catching it, and straight-arming his way into the bathroom.

My traumatic experience had to do with a hair. You see, he and his friends all had apelike chests, covered with what looked like black fur. I, on the other hand, had a chest so small there was room for only one hair on it. I was proud of this hair, and looked admiringly at it each morning while I shaved.

One day, without provocation, my roommate and two of his brawny friends threw me to the floor, sat on me, and bared my chest. My roommate had a straight-edge razor in his hand.

"What are you going to do?" I asked, understandably concerned.

"I'm going to split that hair of yours right down the middle," he said. "That'll give you twice as many hairs as you had before."

And so he did, or tried to do. Maybe he was inexperienced as a hair-splitter. Maybe I wiggled a little. Anyhow, my precious hair was cut off or pulled out.

A few years later, it is true, my chest began to sprout hairs like a newly seeded lawn. But at the time, denuded or deforested, I regretted the loss and was resentful.

This will give you some idea of what may happen in college if a student has a roommate.

Now that I have this autobiographical episode off my chest, let me proceed with other aspects of student life.

Students eat in a large dining hall and too fast. The dining hall is well appointed, with salt and pepper shakers and a bottle of catsup on each table. Food is served cafeteria style, which means that students hungrily push trays ahead of them, point to the things they want, and grunt. It is not hard to decide, because they are faced with the same choice every day.

Professors can size up students by whether they take coffee. Those who take coffee do so to stay awake in class. Those who don't take coffee don't want to stay awake.

The college serves wholesome, body-building food, prepared under the direction of a dietitian who is thoroughly trained and has only the minor physical

The famous string bean riot

handicap of withered taste buds. Students usually take no action about the food other than to complain in a petition to the President. The President acts swiftly, replying within a month that "Your petition has been received and is under study" or "Your petition has been referred to the appropriate committee."

Conditions must have been worse than usual to provoke the famous String Bean Riot of 1936 at a certain Midwestern college. What seems to have set the riot off was a string of twenty-three days of string beans. At last the Dean of Men appeared on a balcony above the cafeteria, looking down on the unruly, milling crowd, and said, "Let them eat cake."

The riot came to an abrupt end, and the Dean's words, sometimes erroneously attributed to Marie Antoinette, became famous.

Students may supplement the college food, at their own expense, with vitamin pills, Tums, and an occasional meal at one of the restaurants downtown.

Near the dormitories and dining hall are recreational facilities. These include a swimming pool where students in the Lifesaving Class are taught that there are other ways to save a drowning person besides yelling "Help!"

Other recreational facilities include baseball and football fields, tennis courts, and archery butts. Archery butts are made of straw, and anyone standing behind one of them is perfectly safe. So is anyone standing directly in front. The danger area is at some distance on either side. "I shot an arrow into the air," said Long-fellow, who had overcut Elementary Archery, was flunking anyhow, and just went through the motions.

The largest crowds gather in the stands at the football field on Saturdays during the football season when the home team is playing at home. The roar of the crowd can be heard for blocks when a long pass is completed or a touchdown is made or the referee is tackled by mistake. Football develops leadership and team spirit. As the Coach once put it, in a between-halves pep talk: "Go in there and fight. If you have to break a leg, break a leg, but don't let the referee see you. Remember the rule book and the ways I've taught you of getting around it."

All colleges, it should be noted, do not give equally high place to football and other rough, competitive sports. Some colleges have de-emphasized football, playing the game in a gentlemanly way and doing their best to keep uniforms from becoming soiled. If they have not won a game in six years, no matter. As the Coach, a Ph.D. in English, said, after a chalk talk in which he compared the split-T formation with the split infinitive: "Let us not be downhearted if we are defeated again tomorrow. We know we are superior to our opponents in the things that count. Surely no member of their team can quote as many lines of *The Wasteland* as our left tackle. Nor can any of them play the cello like our second-string quarterback. So go in there as always, happy in the thought that as soon as the game is over you can return to your books. One final word. At the close of the game, when you form in a circle around the opposing team and sing *Gaudeamus Igitur,* I wish you would enunciate somewhat more clearly than last time."

Football games bring back to the campus old grads who are rich and successful and do not mind letting this be known. However, some of these old grads, especially if they are over fifty, see very little of the game, because they are busy watching the cheer leaders in their tight sweaters and short skirts.

At the far end of the recreation area is a gymnasium, or gym, with a basketball court for holding dances on. This is probably why a dance, especially when it is formal, is called a ball.

Just off the campus are the fraternity and sorority houses, each with two or three Greek letters over the doorway to make visiting Greeks feel right at home. Once a year, on Homecoming Day, these fraternity and sorority houses are decorated in honor of the Greek god, Homecoming. The rest of the year the lawns and porches look empty, with nothing but empty beer cans and empty whisky bottles. Occasionally a fraternity house will seem to have no signs of life about it and there will be a large padlock on the front door. This indicates that the fraternity has been closed for some infraction of the rules, such as having an orgy on campus instead of at a hotel downtown or firing a shotgun over the head of the Dean and wasting ammunition. Sorority houses are seldom closed, because if women break any rules they put them back together again before anyone notices.

An aerial photograph of the campus in winter, covered with snow, looks like this:

VII

EXPENSES

Expenses include room, board, and tuition. (Intuition is left to the student, but anyway it's free.) The total educational cost would be much greater if it were not for endowment and annual gifts. Once the student becomes an alumnus, he is reminded from time to time that he did not really pay as much as he cost the college. It is hoped that these subtle reminders will develop in him a guilt complex. After spending a fortune on psychiatrists, he will find it cheaper to build a gymnasium or endow a chair.

The cost of a room varies, depending on whether it is in one of the newer dormitories and what kind of view it has. Most expensive of all are the rooms in the men's dormitory directly across from the women's dormitory. A few rooms with fireplaces are available for students who wish to sit around roasting wieners, marshmallows, and the administration.

All rooms are tastefully furnished. That is, they contain a bed, a chair, and a desk. Students desiring privacy may put up curtains, while those who optimistically think they will have any time to sleep may bring sheets and a blanket. Maid service is supplied, but it should

Across from the women's dorm

be made clear at the outset that the maids are over sixty and incredibly homely.

Men or women who are married before the end of the semester are required to move to a residence off campus, so they will not corrupt the unmarried students. Exceptions are occasionally made if they keep

their marriage a secret or sign a statement to the effect
that they would be happier not living together. A student who leaves the campus before the end of the semester must forfeit the room deposit. This, more than
anything else, discourages hasty marriages.

In addition to expenses for room, board, and tuition,
there are a few special fees. These include the Applied
Music Fee, payment of which by those who play or
sing gives some satisfaction to students who have to
listen; the Health Fee, which permits students to stick
out their tongues at the College Physician; the Laboratory Fee, giving the student the right to blow himself
up; and the Breakage Fee, which covers the cost of
replacing flasks, test tubes, and windows. Since the
Breakage Fee does not include damage to the student,
an insurance policy is strongly recommended.

A small fee is charged for auditing a course. Auditors,
some of whom are elderly townspeople, attend classes
but are never called on and never take any tests, which
makes them the envy of the regular students.

Miscellaneous fees include the Transcript Fee (which
members of the faculty and administration would gladly
pay out of their own pockets if certain students would
leave) and the fee for field trips. This latter covers the
cost of transportation and, in Geology, the purchase of
non-returnable rocks.

Students with unpaid bills are not graduated. Of
what conceivable use to the college is an alumnus who
is in debt?

VIII

FINANCIAL AID

Financial aid takes many forms, all of them involving money. There are, for example, scholarships. One of these is the Henry M. Humplemeyer Scholarship, established by Henry M. Humplemeyer in memory of Henry M. Humplemeyer, available to any worthy and needy student of good character who comes from North Dakota. Another is the John Doe and Jane Doe Scholarship, given to perpetuate the names of John and Jane Doe by a donor who prefers to remain nameless.

A student applying for a scholarship must show financial need. Parents must submit a statement of resources, and some of the more wealthy have been known to withdraw their checking accounts, register their second Cadillac under the name of a relative, and give up their maid and butler until the scholarship was granted. Such parents, accompanying their offspring for an interview with the Dean of Admissions, usually have their chauffeur drop them off a couple of blocks away, so they can arrive on foot, wearing clothing borrowed from their servants. It is generally acknowledged that no sacrifice is too great to get a college education for one's child without paying for it.

In addition to scholarships there are Loan Funds. These the students must eventually pay back with interest. After graduating, some students lose interest, whereupon the college loses both interest and principal. Other students keep the loan for life, if they are smart, since the college asks only 3 per cent and they can put the money out at 6 per cent, thus making a nice annual profit.

Employment opportunities are available to students who fail to get enough from scholarships and loan funds to make ends meet. One of the most popular forms of employment is waiting tables, though it is hard to see why. Perhaps it is because busboys carry off the dirty dishes and carry on with the girls in the kitchen. Many a beautiful friendship has begun behind the coffee urn. Some will look back on this period as their salad days.

Another popular means of employment is working in the library. At least you don't come away from work with your trouser cuffs full of crumbs. Students working in the library learn technical skills, such as how to turn the little rubber numbers on the date stamp from yesterday's date to today's date, while simultaneously thinking of tonight's date. They also help students find books of reference, books of philosophy, or books of pornography. These they are taught to point out

Beautiful friendship

courteously, for instance "Right in front of you. Can't you read?"

Students who are able to type may augment their income by typing term papers. Since they are paid by the page, student typists soon learn to leave two-inch margins on both the right and left. This also has the advantage of making prose look like poetry.

Once there was a student, whose name it seems best to withhold, who made her way through college without any visible means of support, especially when she wore a strapless evening gown. Though she came of a poor family and was on a scholarship, she lived extravagantly, drinking one Coke after another at the snack bar and buying hardcover books that were available in paperback. There was a rumor that she surprised a certain Professor of Sociology, a married man with four children, in his office one night, and was blackmailing him. Others thought this unlikely, since what on earth would surprise a Professor of Sociology?

At any rate, opportunities of this sort are limited, and no help in finding them may be expected from the Employment Office.

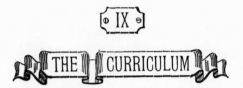

IX

THE CURRICULUM

The purpose of the curriculum is to prepare students to cope with the problems of today. Examples of courses which will be helpful in this regard are "Principles of Hellenistic Art," "French Poetry of the Renaissance," and "Music of the Baroque and Pre-Classical Periods."

To graduate, a student must have acquired 120 units and be able to swim the length of the pool. In acquiring 120 units, it is hoped that the student has learned to think. In swimming the length of the pool, it is hoped that the student has learned to swim. Both of these requirements must be met, since it is not a case of think or swim.

Every student must take a foreign language for two years. This does not mean that the requirement is satisfied after the student has spent two years on First Year French, as the head of the French Department will be glad to explain. Latin will be accepted as satisfying

65

the language requirement, since otherwise not enough students would enroll to justify keeping the Professor of Classics, who has no other way to make a living.

One year of science is also required. It is recommended that students who are poorly prepared in mathematics avoid physics and take botany, in which questions involving mathematics are not likely to go beyond "How many leaves has a four-leaf clover?"

Every student must have a major, or field of concentration. To help select a major, the student is assigned a Faculty Adviser, who shortly afterward goes to some distant place, such as Pakistan, on a research project. The student usually has one meeting with his Adviser, however, and it goes something like this:

> Student: I'm thinking of majoring in English.
> Adviser: Fine.
> Student: Or maybe History.
> Adviser: History's a good subject too.
> Student: My mother thinks I should major in Art.
> Adviser: An excellent idea.
> Student: But my father says Econ would be more practical.
> Adviser: Of course.
> Student: Then there's Political Science.
> Adviser: Yes, there is.
> Student: And Religion, Comparative Literature, and Philosophy.
> Adviser: Quite true.

Student: I appreciate your helping me clarify my thinking.

Adviser: Don't mention it. It's my job. Drop in again in a few months, when I get back from Pakistan.

"Drop in again when I get back from Pakistan"

There are year courses and semester courses. A year course is a course that does a semester's work in a year. A semester course is a course that does a year's work in a semester. Most courses include lectures, when the professor does all the talking, and discussion, when the professor and one student do all the talking. Discussions are intended to develop independent thinking. This means that while the discussion is going on, the students not involved in it are free to think about whatever they want to think about. They are also encouraged to think for themselves. Thinking for others is not permitted by the Honor Code (see below).

For qualified students, there is a program of Independent Study. This permits students to study whatever and whenever and wherever they want to, and may eventually have the same effect on professors as automation is having on factory workers. Students pursuing Independent Study write a long paper or a thesis with a bibliography which lists all the books on the subject they should have used.

For a few outstanding, anti-social students there is what is known as an Honors Program. This is like the program of Independent Study but more so. Students who read for Honors have their own cubicle in the library and read for hours on end. The work may leave its mark on them for life, especially if they sit on a chair with a wicker bottom. Most students who read for Honors go on to graduate school and then into teaching, being incapable of doing anything else.

In addition to term papers, students must expect quizzes and final examinations. One type of quiz is the pop quiz, which is given on a day when no one is prepared. How professors know which day this is is a professional secret. Usually these quizzes are objective, which means that questions can be answered by a single word, such as "Yes" or "No" but not "Maybe." This enables the professor to check on the student's knowledge of facts and, more important, correct the quiz quickly enough to get in eighteen holes before dark.

Final examinations are scheduled well in advance, enabling the student to plan his time carefully and do all the reading for the entire term on the day before. Being more difficult to grade and harder on the eyes than short quizzes, final examinations are read by a graduate assistant.

To get ready for examinations, students are helped by:

1. Hot coffee
2. Cold showers
3. Propping up the eyelids with toothpicks or matches
4. Lucky charms, such as a rabbit's foot (from which the rabbit has been carefully removed)
5. Brisk walks, from which there is a temptation not to return
6. Brains

Courses meet three times a week: Monday, Wednesday, and Friday or Tuesday, Thursday, and an Arranged Hour. The Arranged Hour is a way of avoiding classes on Saturday, which always happens to come on a weekend. Since it is hard to find an hour which is not occupied by Choir Practice, the Arranged Hour is usually omitted, especially by any professor who wants a Student Following.

Science courses have laboratory periods which last all afternoon and conflict with ROTC. Or, as the science professors look at it, ROTC conflicts with their laboratory periods. Students in foreign languages spend a good many hours in the language laboratory, sitting around with headphones and looking like delegates to the UN. Some of the time they are listening to themselves, trying to find out how a foreign language sounds when it is mispronounced.

Art classes are held outdoors, except when students are painting nudes. Of course they do not actually paint nudes, they paint pictures of them. All students do not paint. Some, of a more practical turn, make ceramics which can be used as ash trays or doorstops. Each spring there is a student art show when student works are admired and sometimes purchased by parents and friends. From the throng of art lovers can be heard such discerning questions as "What is that supposed to be?" and "How much is it?"

Plays are put on under the supervision of the Drama Department. Students who act or paint scenery or sell tickets stay up late at night drinking coffee and growing beards. All play and no work brings down their grades but seems worth it until they read the review by the local drama critic, a man who, having once written a play which has never been produced, is considered (by himself) an expert. "It was a farce," he writes, if the play was a tragedy, or "It was a tragedy," if the play was a farce. He is not hard to identify in a crowd, for he twirls his cane and wears his topcoat like a cape.

The drama coach, like the football coach, gives the members of the cast a pep talk between acts. Instead of "Get in there and fight," he says, "Don't be so wooden, or the scene shifters will move you off with the furniture." He has a great sense of humor, as long as he is making fun of someone else. Everyone knows he was on Broadway once, as a young man, but few know he was at the corner of Broadway and 42nd, giving away free tickets for a Radio City tour.

When the students put on a production of *Hamlet*, the auditorium is always filled, since attendance is required by English teachers in the local high school. The teachers themselves do not have to attend, however, since they have seen *Hamlet* before. Many who are seeing a Shakespeare play for the first time are amazed at how long it is.

The highlight of Geology and Botany are the field trips to collect specimens. Since rocks do not wither, like flowers and plants, and make better paperweights, Geology has its advantages. But students who like to press flowers between the pages of a book find Botany preferable. After-dark field trips, to see night-blooming flora, are especially popular in coeducational institutions. (Flora could, of course, be the name of a girl who just really gets going after sundown.)

Field trips are not confined to science. Practical experience is gained in Sociology and Government by visiting prisons, insane asylums, and meetings of the local city council. In this way students are encouraged to take an interest in community activities.

Once a professor, taking a class in Social Psychology to a home for juvenile delinquents, left one of the students behind. By the time the boy's absence was discovered, he had become a ward of the state, and legal maneuvering to return him to college dragged into the second semester. "I usually count the students before entering an institution and again afterwards," the professor said later. "This time I must have goofed."

The various fields of study are divided into departments. Without departments, there would be no chance for a faculty member to become chairman of the department with a higher salary and less teaching. Department chairmen recommend appointments and promotion and therefore hold the whip hand (in which there only *seems* to be a whip) over junior faculty members, who try to ingratiate themselves in little ways. An energetic and imaginative young Instructor in English of our acquaintance used to wash the chairman's car. An Assistant Professor shopped at the same supermarket as the chairman's wife and pushed her cart. He expected to be promoted to Associate Professor but wound up as corespondent in a messy divorce case.

It is not customary for a department chairman to

A department chairman

wear a crown or sit on a throne, but this is a matter of personal preference.

The departments are grouped in divisions: Humanities, Social Studies, and Natural and Physical Sciences. Whether Psychology is a Natural Science or an Unnatural Science is open to question. ROTC, or Military Science, is probably a Natural Science, because it is perfectly natural to want to kill people. It is hard to know where to put Philosophy and History, Philosophy involving thinking deeply and History involving thinking for a long time. To bring out this distinction between depth and breadth, philosophers should have a

sign over their desk reading
$$\begin{matrix} T \\ H \\ I \\ N \\ K \end{matrix}$$
while historians should

have a sign reading T H I N K.

There is a friendly rivalry among departments as well as divisions over such matters as the number of majors and the size of the book budget. Instead of saying, "My father is richer than your father" or "My brother can lick your brother," a department chairman's child says, "My father's department has more majors than your father's department." To which the other department chairman's child replies, "My old man's department could have as many majors as your old man's if the work were as easy." The first department chairman's child come backs with "Oh, yeah?" and from there it escalates to fisticuffs.

Except for the time an Associate Professor of German was found dead with a volume of Modern French Poetry crammed down his throat, disputes are settled amicably. Usually the appearance of the Dean of the Faculty, at the height of the altercation, suffices. The Dean wears a navy blue suit with a whisk broom instead of a handkerchief in his breast pocket, and has always just cut himself shaving. His appearance is enough to distract anyone.

Students are encouraged to broaden their interests and take work in departments other than that of their major. After completing the English, foreign language, physical education, and science requirements, as well as the state requirement in American history and government, the various prerequisites and advanced courses in the field of concentration, a senior thesis, and a weekly letter to his mother, the student who uses his time well may be able to squeeze in a one-semester elective for the purpose of exploration and the broadening of horizons. This does not apply, however, to premedical students, whose schedule is too tight to permit wasting time on cultural nonessentials, or to transfer students, who for two years concentrated on a different set of requirements at another institution.

The state requirement in American history and government may be fulfilled either by passing an examination or by taking some such course as Patriotism 26a, b or the seminar in Advanced Flag Waving. The examination, calculated to insure that the student knows the basic facts about the American Way of Life, contains such questions as:

1. Can you throw a dollar across a river? Do you think money went farther in Washington's day?

2. Is it true that Theodore Roosevelt was a Bull Moose? Have we elected any other animals to the Presidency?

3. Are cameras for sale, or only for rent, in a bicameral legislature?

4. Have you ever seen anyone take the Fifth Amendment? Did he bring it back?

It might be interesting, at the close of this chapter, to explain the derivation of the word *curriculum*. It comes, like so many long words, from Latin. The Latin word *curriculum* means either a race course or a chariot, which explains why a Roman sometimes found himself driving a *curriculum* around a *curriculum*, all the while marvelling at the economy of the language. *Curriculum*, in turn, comes from *currere*, to run, which is a good thing to do if you see a *curriculum* coming straight at you. The plural of *curriculum* is either *curriculums* or *curricula*, and there are those to whom this makes a great deal of difference.

X

ATTENDANCE

Class attendance is expected of all students, but not of professors. It is customary for students to wait five minutes after the bell. If the professor has not arrived by then, they may safely assume he is ill, has forgotten, or has not read the assignment. Students carefully synchronize their watches. Then, when someone signals that the five minutes are up, one of their number yells, "Go!" Since speed and quiet are of the essence, many students wear tennis shoes or, as they are aptly called, "sneakers." The professor who arrives five minutes and ten seconds after the bell may find two or three students still in the classroom, slowly regaining consciousness after being trampled on.

Regulation of attendance is the prerogative of the professor. That is, he may use whatever means he sees fit to penalize non-attendance. However, the administration frowns on threats of violence, since a professor loses face when he is unable to carry them out. He looks pretty ridiculous when, at the moment of inflicting the penalty, he can't remember where he left his horsewhip. "Has anyone seen my horsewhip?" he asks, and

Five minutes after the bell

even the student bending over feels a little sorry for the forgetful old fuddy-duddy.

A professor of Psychology once made use of hypnotism. At the first meeting of the class, when everyone, not yet realizing how dull the course was going to be, was there, he made the students repeat over and over, while he shone a flashlight into their eyes, "I will be back in this room at 10:00 o'clock on Wednesday. I will be back in this room at 10:00 o'clock on Wednesday." Unfortunately, he failed to say Wednesday *morning*. About half the class tried to get into the locked building at 10:00 o'clock Wednesday evening, and there were splintered doors and broken windows which the professor found it hard to explain to the campus police.

Some professors call the roll at the beginning of each class, students answering "Here" or "Not here" as the case may be. When a student is absent, the professor marks an "a," which is not the same as an "A," in his classbook opposite the student's name. Once, when a student got five "a's" in a row, an absent-minded professor startled the class by shouting "Bingo!"

Instead of calling the roll, some professors seat students alphabetically and know who is absent by the empty seats, unless the absentee can afford to hire a student to sit in his place. This comes to around two dollars an hour, with time-and-a-half for Saturday classes or if the substitute is called on to recite.

Still other professors pretend not to care whether students come to class or not. This is the Mature Attitude, adopted by professors on tenure. A few professors actually hope students won't attend, especially the smart ones who are always asking questions they can't answer. Then again, they may simply have a fear of crowds.

XI

THE GRADING SYSTEM

Grades are A, B, C, D, E, F, FF, and Inc. A is Excellent, and is almost the only grade given by professors of Art and Music and those whose heart begins to show as they near retirement.

A professor giving mostly A's is known to give a "pipe" course, perhaps because anything goes in the classroom, including smoking. True, such a professor may attract only A students, or teach so well that even the dumbest students honestly make an A. However his colleagues, who loudly proclaim (when he is out of hearing) that he is lowering standards and "cheapening the A," doubt this. From the standpoint of such a professor, one of the best things about giving A's is that it is never necessary to argue with students who think they have been treated unfairly.

To offset the professor who gives only A's, there is the one who never gives an A or only rarely, such as when some student discovers that the way to the professor's heart is through his ego. Even then it is not easy, because looking admiringly at the professor and making gushy remarks about his intellect may be taken for flattery.

Usually it is the young instructor who never gives an A, because he is afraid of getting a reputation for giving a pipe course. When a student wonders why he didn't get an A on an examination, after answering every question correctly, the instructor draws himself up to his full height (about five feet eight) and says, "*I give the*

"*I give the grades around here, Mr. Grigsby*"

grades around here, Mr. Grigsby. If you don't like the way I grade, take some other course," forgetting for the moment that this is a required course and the only section that fits into Grigsby's schedule. But it makes him feel better, or at least bigger.

Of course there was the young instructor who had the son of a wealthy trustee in his course in Analytic Geometry, which gave little leeway for subjectivity in grading. It worried this well-meaning young fellow, who was torn between giving the student a C, which he barely deserved, or an A, which might make a lot of nice people happy.

He envied instructors in Sociology, who could give thirty per cent extra for campus activities, or Cultural Involvement. He envied instructors in English, who could give extra points for each word spelled correctly. He considered adding a little something for neatness, except that the boy was incredibly sloppy.

Then it came to him. The student knew more in May than he had known in September, didn't he? A little, anyhow? That was it: Improvement. At once he sensed that he was learning the academic ropes, catching onto the rules of the game. As he gave the trustee's son one of his precious A's, he felt that warm glow of satisfaction within him that comes occasionally to the good teacher.

B is Very Good or, to professors, Very Convenient. A professor who gives all B's is not likely to be accused of lowering standards, except during a comparative study by the *ad hoc* Committee on Grades, made about once in ten years. In fact he can pride himself on almost never giving an A, and make snide remarks about his bird-brained colleagues who do. Moreover, even outstanding students are not likely to embarrass him by asking him to explain why they got a B instead of an A. Their records are so good that they can stand a few B's and still make Phi Beta Kappa. Besides, he can differentiate between the excellent, average, and poor students in his class by giving them B plus, B, or B minus. This permits him a considerable range.

C is Average, though it really isn't.

D is Below Average, and it really is. One D amidst a string of A's and B's, perhaps in Physical Education, looks terrible.

Once there was a student who got a D in Art. The instructor had asked him to draw a bead, and he whipped out a revolver. Had the firing pin not jammed, he might have done even worse in the course.

E is Condition, and the condition is almost always bad. Students who tell their parents that the E on their report means Excellent may get away with it if their parents are also stupid.

F is Failure. An F can be brought up to a D if the student takes a make-up examination, writes an extra paper, or gets something on the professor. However you look at it, an F is not a very good grade.

FF is a Failure That Cannot Be Made Up. It is something like death. You would think the grade after

F would be G, but FF is thought to be more final, like beriberi, which is probably twice as bad as beri. The FF is given by professors who have acid instead of blood in their veins. The only professor ever known to

He gave up teaching

have given all FF's gave up teaching after a year and became a pig-sticker at a slaughterhouse.

Inc. is Incomplete, indicating that the student left the campus suddenly, perhaps to have a baby, despite the considerateness of the college in establishing a nine-month academic year. When the student has made up the necessary work, the grade of Inc. is replaced by whatever grade has been earned in the course, for instance an F.

How do professors determine grades? Many, at least according to students, use an Ouija board. Others prefer a dowsing rod. One professor, a classicist, uses a counting-out rhyme in Latin, after praying to Minerva and sacrificing one of his neighbor's cats. Probably the most widespread and satisfactory method is for the professor to turn the whole nasty business over to his wife.

Occasionally a modern, progressive professor will call the student into his office for a conference.

"What grade do you think you should get?" the professor asks.

"I've never really given it a thought," the student says shyly, dropping his eyes.

"Come, come. You must have some idea," the professor urges.

"Would a B be too high?"

"I'm asking you. You had the course in Standards and Values, didn't you?"

"Yes, and I also took Man and Society and Principles and Ethics."

"Good. Then you should have no trouble deciding."

"Would an A be all right?"

"Whatever you say. After all, it's *your* grade. And fill out this form and take it to the Registrar, please."

"What's it for?"

"It's a descriptive comment that accompanies your grade. Use phrases like 'Outstanding student, conscientious and cooperative.' Just don't make it too long."

"I'll be glad to take care of it."

"One more thing."

"What's that?"

"Don't forget to sign my name."

Grade reports are sent to the student, with a copy to the parents, at the end of each semester. Students who remove their grade report from the mailbox, so that it will not get to their parents, are committing a federal offense but consider it worth while.

"After all," as the Dean says in his annual talk to incoming students, "grades aren't everything. The main thing is to learn."

One thing students learn is what low grades do to your chances of getting a scholarship, not to mention your eligibility for football.

XII

THE HONOR CODE

The Honor Code is not to be confused with the Morse Code. In fact the two are just the opposite, since the Morse Code is used to communicate information to others, while the Honor Code is used to keep it to oneself.

Students are on their honor not to cheat. The worst thing about cheating is that the student may get away with it in the classroom and then a few years later, overconfident, go in for cheating on a large scale, such as embezzling a million dollars, and get caught. The penalty for this turns out to be a good deal harsher than an F and three weeks of encampusment. As Pope said, "A little cheating is a dangerous thing."

Sometimes on examination papers and bluebooks students are asked to write "I pledge on my honor that I have neither given nor received help," followed by their signature. It is more blessed to receive than to give. Anyone who gives help, running all that risk and

89

getting nothing out of it, is so stupid it's a wonder he knows anything in the first place.

Students can be inventive and ingenious about cheating. One student brought a transistor radio to an examination in Religions of the World, ostensibly to listen to a ball game. Actually he received a stream of information on the Buddhists, Shintoists, Hindus, Confucianists, Taoists, Moslems, etc. from his roommate, who was at the college radio station with the textbook. By using earphones, he considerately kept from distracting other students or the proctor.

Proctors, too, can make use of modern electronic devices for detection. Not only do they keep the class under constant surveillance with high-powered binoculars, through a one-way window, but they communicate by walkie-talkie whenever they spot anything out of line.

"Suspicious markings on cuff of boy in second row, third in from aisle. Over."

"Roger. Am using infra-red telescopic scanner. Over."

"Advise what you find. Over."

"Markings appear to be note to blonde in next seat. A little hard to make out, but I think it reads: 'You look good enough to eat. Munch, munch. Remember we have a date at the Dirty Spoon tonight.' Over."

"Probably all right, but it might be code. Keep your eyes peeled for any papers passed under desk, and intercept. Over."

"Roger."

Professors can, of course, make cheating virtually impossible by avoiding objective tests. All they have to do is to lead the student into an essay-type answer with something like "Discuss the philosophic issues involved in an understanding of social activity, with special emphasis on freedom and predictability, objectivity, causality, and relations between the individual and society." Faced with the prospect of reading thirty or forty examination papers on such a topic, professors may be forgiven if they start their examination: "Answer the following Yes or No" or "Place a check mark in the appropriate square."

One rather subtle form of cheating is plagiarism, or writing papers copied out of books which it is hoped the instructor has not read. An instructor who finds the prose style in a freshman theme somewhat unusual for a freshman, may think it sounds like Arnold J. Toynbee. After doing a great deal of reading, and learning a remarkable lot of history, he discovers it is from William Babington Macaulay. Despite all the work he has gone to, it was worth it to be able to write on the paper: "This was obviously taken verbatim from Macaulay." Then, with the finely honed sarcasm of which professors frequently avail themselves, confident that students will not dare reply in kind: "If you had to steal something, you should have stolen something with which I was not familiar, if possible." The student, too busy being rushed by a fraternity to write his own paper, gets an F in the course and, at the end of the year, drops out of college, while the professor's reputation for omniscience gets a big boost.

What the student will never know is that the professor's doctoral dissertation was made up almost entirely of deftly interwoven passages from two or three obscure nineteenth-century historians. However the professor, thanks to techniques learned in graduate school, knew how to use *ibid.*, *op. cit.*, *loc. cit.*, and *passim* in his footnotes so effectively that it was impossible for anyone to track down his references. Also the graduate professor who supervised his doctoral dissertation was too busy with his own research to do any sleuthing.

The simplest way to prepare a term paper without writing it is to have it done by an agency that specializes in this sort of thing. For a small sum, say a hundred dollars, you can get a ten-page paper written on any subject, with a grade of B or better guaranteed. However, one student who had his paper written for him by such an outfit was guilty not only of cheating but of gross negligence. When he turned in his paper, he forgot and left in the bill.

Under the Honor Code, of course, a student would not think of cheating. Or he might think about it and promptly dismiss the idea as unworthy. There is too much risk of being caught. And being caught means being brought before the Judiciary Board, a group of students who are so smart they don't need to cheat. Most students would rather flunk, or even study hard enough to pass honestly, than face the Judiciary Board.

The Board takes up not only cheating but cases of immoral and anti-social behavior, such as drunkenness and sexual promiscuity—not because these things are wrong but because they may, if overdone, give the college a bad name.

To summarize, the Honor Code is a great help. Without it, things would be worse.

XIII

THE DEGREE

On completion of the required course of studies, the student is given the B.A. or, if he has avoided all impractical courses, the B.S. He is now entitled to put his degree after his name, like an M.D., but will be subjected to considerable ridicule if he does, unless he lives in England.

The degree is proof of the fact that the student is Educated, despite doubts raised by his inability to write clearly, keep his bank account balanced, or be logical in an argument. When people ask him, "Where did you go?" he is able to tell where he went.

The degree is formally conferred at Commencement, the final test of the student's stamina and fortitude. Commencement takes place in June, the weather determining whether it is held indoors or outdoors. If it is held indoors, in the college gym, which is without air conditioning and smells of sweat socks, it will be the hottest day of the year, while if it is held outdoors there will be a steady downpour, beginning almost the instant the College Chaplain opens the ceremony with the invocation. Possibly what sounds like "Let us spray" is heard by some ancient rain god.

Students wear academic robes, which are black because students are supposed to be in mourning at having to leave college after four happy years of examinations, term papers, and required physical education. On their heads are mortarboards, a type of headgear which has never caught on for everyday use. While the glee club is singing, a wind inevitably rises and students must hold onto their mortarboards or graduate bareheaded.

The faculty, which could not otherwise find its way, is led by the Faculty Marshal. The Marshal carries a mace, a heavy staff about five feet long which is a reminder to faculty members that they had better not get out of step. In the early days, the mace had spikes on the end, but these were removed as the result of pressure from the AAUP.

After the invocation by the Chaplain and one number too many by the glee club, the President introduces the commencement speaker, who is either (1) another college President, who, by reciprocal arrangement, is willing to speak for nothing if he is given an honorary degree, (2) the head of a large corporation, educational foundation, or other source of funds, or (3) a graduate of the college who has been more successful than anyone would have dreamed.

The President's introduction of the commencement speaker is full of facts everyone has been dying to know, such as where he went to college, professional societies to which he belongs, his participation in such community activities as the Chamber of Commerce (vice president, 1949) and the Community Chest (chairman for his block, 1952), his publications (including his widely read "Structural Relationships of Pteridophytes and Seed Plants"), his military service, his travels, his hobbies, and his golf handicap. Mainly the President is trying to justify his selection of the speaker, especially

The Marshal and his mace

since the fiasco of last year, when the speaker was told not to exceed twenty minutes and spoke slightly over an hour and was extremely dull, except for an off-color story that offended several of the wealthiest trustees.

The following words, phrases, and inspiring statements will be useful to any commencement speaker. By putting them together, in any order, the speaker will have a speech which, when he has concluded, the President will characterize as "a brilliant and memorable address":

"You of the younger generation"
"The future is in your hands"
"Liberty"
"Freedom"
"Your place in society"
"Can you hear me?"
"The whole man"
"Leaders of tomorrow"
"Changing values"
"We of our generation will not live to see"
"History teaches us"
"As you go forth"
"You young people"
"That reminds me of the story about"
"Our great country"
"There must be something wrong with the microphone"
"Challenge of our times"
"In conclusion"
"Technological advance"

"The world we live in"
"When I was in college"
"Members of the graduating class"
"Looking ahead"
"To sum up"
"This great institution"
"Your distinguished President"
"God"
"In the words of Thomas Jefferson"
"You will recall Shakespeare's lines"
"If I may take just a few more minutes"

The bright spot of most commencement addresses is when the speaker's notes blow off the lectern.

When the speaker has concluded and there is no further way to prolong the ceremony, the President reluctantly proceeds to confer the degrees. Handing each student a diploma with his right hand and shaking hands with his left, until he realizes there is something awkward about this, the President says over and over, "By virtue of the authority vested in me by the Board of Trustees, I confer upon you the degree of Bachelor of Arts." Now and then his tongue gets slightly twisted and it comes out "By virtue of the vest authorized me by the Toard of Bustees. . . ."

At this point one trustee leans over to another and whispers, "Isn't the Prexy getting pretty close to retirement?"

At some colleges the Dean of the Faculty then takes hold of the tassel on the student's mortarboard and moves it from the right side to the left. At other colleges the student is permitted to do this for himself, as a sign of his having reached a level of intellectual maturity and physical coordination when he can do such things on his own. In any case, the tassel which previously had bothered the student by dangling in his right eye, now bothers him by dangling in his left eye.

Some trustees think this shift from the right to the left is part of the Communist conspiracy. "I'm not saying any of the faculty are card-carrying Communists," they mutter open-mindedly, "but altogether too many of them are from Harvard."

Now that they have their degrees, students are ready

to go out into the world, where they have not been, except summers, for four years. Great Choices and Important Decisions face them. With a woman, it is a choice between marriage and a career, unless she is so unattractive that this is already decided for her. With a man, it is a choice between graduate school, military service, and a job. No wonder the graduate schools are filled to capacity.

XIV

FACULTY AND STAFF

As it says in one of the promotional brochures, "More important to the college than its buildings or its curriculum are the dedicated people who make up its faculty and staff." Most members of the faculty and staff are dedicated, all right, but not like the current yearbook, which is "Dedicated to Ellie Mae Crump, Champion of Freedom." Ellie Mae, it should be explained, was a cooperative member of the dormitory staff, no longer with the college, who for a small consideration permitted several hundred copies to be made of her master key.

Once, it is true, a faculty member dedicated himself in writing. This man, a bachelor with a classic profile which he obligingly turned first this way and then that, to give his students a good view, died suddenly. Some thought his untimely end was caused by exhausting vigils in front of a mirror. Others were of the opinion that he starved himself to death, trying to keep his 30-

inch waistline. At any rate, since he was fond of quoting Browning's

> Open my heart, and you will see
> Graved inside of it, "Italy,"

as a reminder to everyone that he spent a sabbatical year in Perugia, the physician who attended him asked for an autopsy. He had a hunch, and he was right. Engraved on this dedicated professor's heart was a single word, "Me." It could easily have caused his demise.

Let us now examine the key people (so called be-

The key people

cause most possess a Phi Beta Kappa key) without whom the college would not be what it is today—struggling with a deficit and about to lose its accreditation.

First there is the Trustee. He is one of thirty-six members of a self-perpetuating Board. Self-perpetuating means that most trustees remain in office for life, and even longer. Though words do not fail me, prose does, and I therefore turn to verse:

Trustee

He seldom makes the meeting in the fall;
An afternoon in spring, at best, is all
The time he has to give to education,
So busy is he with his corporation.
And if his watch is often in his hand,
The other gentlemen will understand
That though it is, admittedly, a pity,
He has important business in the city.
So, having been assured there are no Reds
And shaken hands with all department heads
And heard the Prexy's hopeful parting bit
About a way to end the deficit,
He leaves the academic scene behind
And shortly puts it safely out of mind.
His name, they say, is one that carries weight
When listed in the catalogue, and fate
And taxes willing, doubtless will appear
Upon a building almost any year.

The President is appointed by the Trustees and serves, according to the charter of the college, "at their pleasure." He tries his best to please them or at least to fool them. Since Trustees, fortunately, are usually not educators, the latter is rather easy for any President worth his salt. On retirement, a college President has an excellent chance of becoming a consultant to an educational foundation. An educational foundation is about the only organization, except a government agency, which has so much money that it is able to pay for advice it has no intention of using.

President

He has such perquisites as these:
An inside track to LL.D.s,
A large and handsome rent-free house,
A part-time maid to help his spouse,
A special fund for entertaining,
Fare paid (first class) whenever planing,
Two secretaries well equipped—
Sharp minded and sharp pencil-tipped—
Guest memberships in sundry clubs,
With steam baths and relaxing rubs—
Much else, in fact too much to mention,
Besides a quite substantial pension.

What does he do to earn all these?
He merely pacifies trustees
And students, faculty, old grads,
Townspeople, also Moms and Dads,

And keeps his health and keeps his sanity
And isn't heard to use profanity,
And, living in a goldfish bowl,
Next day can be filet of sole:
Unlike professors whom he hires
He has no tenure, walks on wires,
And if he falls, he's out, he's gone,
While they—some sad, some glad—stay on.

Colleges have many deans, not to mention associate deans, assistant deans, and people like Dean Rusk, Dean Acheson, and Dean Chance. But the top dean, or top dog, whose bite is worse than his bark, is the Dean of the Faculty. Frequently the Dean is "recruited" from

Acting dean

the local faculty, which does not mean that a bugle is sounded and he has to go, after a tearful scene with his wife and children. Sometimes a Dean is "brought in from the outside," which means exactly what it seems to mean. When the Dean leaves suddenly in the middle of the year, because of a nervous breakdown, a morals charge, or whatever, someone is given the position temporarily and assumes the title of Acting Dean. He tries his best to act like a Dean.

Though the Dean is said to be "of the Faculty," he is really "of the Administration." He is against the faculty, or so at least some of the faculty believe. In some ways he is a pathetic figure:

Dean of the Faculty

When he considers how his days are spent
(More than professor, not quite president,
Though toward the latter tentatively reaching),
He wonders if he should have left his teaching.
Of course—he rubs his high, impressive brow—
He has a private secretary now
And sits upon the platform in the spring,
Crown prince and heir apparent, though not king.
And while some whisper that it must be four,
He really makes a good two thousand more
From what is called the administrative racket
Than any in the full professor bracket.

And yet, with summer just ahead, he dreams
Of bygone days—how one month hardly seems

Enough (as three months did) for going places.
He longs, too, for those rows of student faces,
More cheerful than committeemen. (You know,
The Dean is always *ex officio.*)
He notices the dust that thickens on
The box of three-by-fives. He has not gone
Inside to add a note on Chaucer's *-e,*
Last chapter of his book, since '53.

So he considers how his days are spent,
More than professor, not quite president.

As might have been mentioned earlier, the word
dean comes from the Latin *decanus,* or chief of ten,
and originally referred to a person who was the head
over ten monks. The Dean of Men has many more than
ten persons under him, and none of them bears much
resemblance to a monk. Sometimes the Dean tries to
be "one of the boys," and says to the students, "Call
me Jim." The students don't know whether they really
should. They think he is trying to worm something out
of them, and they are right. Here he is:

Dean of Men

A summons from the Dean of Men
Strikes terror into nine of ten.
The tenth—unpale, untense, undrawn—
Works for the Dean. He mows his lawn.

But why be frightened of him, really?
Behind that voice so stern and steely,

Behind those X-ray eyes all-seeing
There is a human human being,

A man of flesh and blood and bones
Who laughs and cries and even moans
And has that necessary part
He sometimes seems to lack, a heart.

A kindly man, his friends say, though
Of course a student wouldn't know.

The opposite number of the Dean of Men is the Dean of Women, a middle-aged woman who is usually a spinster or a widow. Sometimes, though rarely, she has a husband, a man who skulks around the house and is happiest in the garden, puttering with the petunias or raking the mulch heap. The Dean of Women, as is often said, "has her hands full." If she didn't, you could see how her nails are bitten to the quick. There must be some other way to make a living, but, perhaps because of masochistic tendencies, she stays with it:

Dean of Women

She never married. Many wonder why.
When she was young, did young men pass her by?
Or did she spurn them all, the weak and strong,
And wait for someone else, and wait too long?

A dean, but also mother-image, friend,
Girls bring their broken hearts for her to mend.
They bring their problems mountain large, their ills,

And ask that she make mountains into hills.
She "holds up moral standards" and will fight
A rearguard battle if she thinks she's right,
Will face, indeed, the very hordes of Hades
If this would make young women into ladies.

She goes to College Church, sits where she's seen,
To set a good example as the Dean.
The sign says "By Appointment" on her door,
And every year she drinks a little more.

As for the next administrative officer, this is about all
that needs to be said:

Dean of Admissions

Here is, perhaps, the lowest dean,
The last in line, though first one seen
By students come from every sector.
(Sometimes this dean is called Director.)

This is the dean that mans the gate
Like Peter, possibly, or Fate,
And lets some in and keeps some out,
Yet never has (or shows) a doubt.

This dean's a strainer, sieve, or filter,
And very rarely out of kilter.
He therefore loses face, in hunks,
Each time a prize admittee flunks.

At home you have a closet to stuff stuff into. At colleges they have a Registrar's Office. Presiding over this

is the Registrar. Though she is about the same height and width as a filing cabinet, you can easily tell which one she is. She is the one without handles down the front. The Registrar has the low-down on everyone, present and past, and is counting the days until retirement, when she plans to open a small blackmailing business. Meet this character:

Registrar

An academic CPA,
She keeps the records day by day
And year by year in strict sequester,
And measures time out by semester.
Safe in a safe and filed in files
Are papers which, on end, for miles
Would stretch, would reach the moon or Mars
Or possibly the outer stars.

She leaves to scholars, Ph.D.s,
Interpretations, theories.
Her field is figures, facts, statistics.
No truck has she with moody mystics.
She knows the regulations cold,
And none there is who'd be so bold
As to remark, or hint, she errs.
No pen or tongue's as sharp as hers.

She meets with facts each stratagem,
And prays each night to IBM.

The Alumni Director is sometimes called the Alumni Secretary, just as alumni are sometimes called alumnae,

depending on their sex. But this is less important than
what an alumna is called when she has married and di-
vorced. Is she using the name of her ex-husband or her
maiden name? A change of name or of address is something that is usually discovered just after the Alumni
Directory has gone to press and there will not be another for ten years. The Alumni Director wishes alumni
would stay married and stay put. Also, if it is not too
much to ask, he wishes they would let him know when
they die, so he can give them some publicity in the
obituary column of the Newsletter. Look out—here he
comes:

Alumni Director

Although their number grows each year that passes,
He knows alumni by their names and classes
As well as occupations, where they live,
And what (not half enough) each year they give.
At every football game you'll hear him scream
As loud as any student, "Team! Go! Team!"
For Alma Mater he will do or die.
He wears her sacred colors in his tie.

The college is his meat and drink, his life.
He loves it as he does his children, wife.
And since he's willed it half his earthly store,
The pity is they do not pay him more.

Faculty meetings are on the second Tuesday of each
month, whether there is any business to transact or not.
Oddly, the less business there is, the longer the meet-

Alumni director

ing. Those who have never attended a faculty meeting wouldn't understand. But for those who have:

Faculty Meeting

Convened, except for those who make it a point
    of honor
To be late and thus thought busy,
At four;
Adjourned, after dispatching half an hour's business,
At six,
Scholars, dispassionate and logical in articles for
    the learned journals,
Become passionate and illogical on departmental
    budgets,
On promotion and tenure,
And on a change in the wording of section five,
    paragraph three, subparagraph two
Of regulations regarding class attendance;
Patient searchers after truth by means of Bunsen
    burners, microfilms, and the interlibrary loan—
Honest men, modest men, fearless men—open their
    coats
To bare their Phi Beta Kappa keys,
Clear their throats importantly, move, second the
    motion, and with a faint remembrance of
    Robert's Rules of Order
Call for the question after a furtive look at their
    watches.
Faculty members individually
Are people.

Faculty members collectively
Are faculty members.

A Professor Emeritus is to a college what a Chairman
of the Board is to a corporation. He has been kicked
upstairs, and if he tries to sneak back down, he is kicked
right up again. The main difference between a Professor Emeritus and a Chairman of the Board is that a
Professor Emeritus owns no stock. "Emeritus," by the
way, literally means "out of merit," which is about right:

Professor Emeritus

Though many thought it somewhat late,
He felt that he, at sixty-eight,
Was at his best and barely reaching
The summit of his college teaching.
You do not cut the plant down when
It starts to bloom, so pray why then
Rip out the teacher firm of root
For some green, spindly substitute?
But rules are rules, the president
Had said, and thoughtful students sent
A "first" of Yeats, and with it wrapped
A note signed "Seniors" which so tapped
Near dried-up ducts that tears came welling,
Despite mistakes they made in spelling.
Some shook his hand who had not shaken
It since the year that sides were taken
On giving up requirements in
The ancient languages—a sin

He felt it then and feels it still,
Dead languages that none can kill. . . .
Last class, last wistful look around
The bookless office, bells' last sound,
These were the painful moments, though
He still will be nearby, you know;
He lives in town, he'll come to teas
And watch conferring of degrees
And meet old students who will say
He looks exactly as the day
They knew him first, and he will beam
And go back home to doze and dream.

Most professors are married and therefore, inescapably, have a wife. If very few professors have more than one wife, this is not so much because it is against the regulations as because it is too expensive. Of course sometimes a faculty member's wife works, perhaps as a schoolteacher or as a receptionist in a dentist's office, and earns more than her husband. You can guess how he feels: grateful for this extra income. A wife can help her husband in the academic world, not only by working but by entertaining graciously and by passing along important bits of gossip. That is why, when a professor is looked over before being hired, the President also carefully looks over his wife, and if she is pretty, over and over. Sometimes a professor jokingly refers to his wife as "my better half," when everyone knows it is more like two thirds:

Because of her

Faculty Wife

She keeps him fed and warm and mended,
  Reminds him of appointments,
And when he slips and falls, upended,
  Applies the proper ointments.

She types his speeches, notes, reviews,
  Reads proof, and checks each reference.
She finds his misplaced overshoes
  And treats his Dean with deference.

She's treasurer of Campus Wives
　　And chairman of her section.
She goes from door to door on drives.
　　Her dinners are perfection.

Her husband's something of a dud,
　　He's uninspired and narrow.
His veins are rather lacking blood,
　　His bones are short of marrow.

He plods along from day to day,
　　Accepting her devotion,
And it's because of her, they say,
　　He got his last promotion.

　　No one really knows whether it is students or professors who have the greater dislike for early classes.
The only thing worse than early classes is Saturday
classes, or early classes on Saturday. Unless, to be sure,
it is classes just before lunch, when stomachs growl
menacingly. Or just after lunch, when there is an over-
whelming urge to lie down. If the professor feels drow-
siness coming on, he need only write a few questions on
the blackboard and, honoring the honor system, walk
out of the classroom and up to his office, where he
keeps a sofa for just such an emergency.
　　As for early classes, this happens to be one in English
Poetry of the Nineteenth Century, though it could just
as well be in Introduction to Philosophy or Principles
of Economics:

Eight O'clock Class

Three times a week this small assembly meets,
With drooping eyelids and half-hidden yawn,
To hear, incredulous, how Shelley, Keats,
And Wordsworth rose to write before the dawn.

A Department Head is the same as a Department Chairman, except to a Department Head. One should never make the mistake of a book salesman, formerly a Navy man, who asked, "Where is the Department head?" and was directed to the Department Head when he was really looking for the men's room. Imagine his dismay when he opened the door and was told by a secretary to wait, the Head was busy. Usually it takes years of teaching, publishing, and keeping out of trouble to become a Department Head. The only exception is in such a field as Classics, in a small college. Since there is only one person in the department, competition is at a minimum. If you think the Department Head in Classics envies the Department Head in Sociology, who has six faculty members under him, you may be right.

There are, I am told, exceptions to the following:

Department Head

He counts the majors in his field
   And checks his closest rival.
More majors mean more funds for books,
More staff, more awed, respectful looks,
   Or anyhow survival.

At times he's politic, and then
　　At times no one's inepter.
But he is always at the helm,
And since he rules his little realm
　　Should have a crown and scepter.

Many colleges have a policy known as Publish or Perish. This explains the existence of scholarly journals, which give the author ten offprints of his article. One

The alternative to publishing

he gives to the President, one to the Dean of the Faculty, one to the Department Head, one he keeps for himself, and the other six he sends to scholars in his field, who will file it away unread, in return for articles they have sent him which he filed away unread. The alternative to publishing (perishing) will not be discussed here. So, onward and upward:

Professor's Progress

Each article he wrote, though paper thin
(And thinner still, if truth be known, within),
He placed upon the one he wrote before,
A slowly rising pile upon the floor.
Each tiniest addendum, near ethereal,
Dredged out of desiccated source material,
He placed upon the others there below
And proudly watched the paper pillar grow.
Then mounting quickly with expectant smile
And careful step the scholar's precious pile,
He stood at last triumphant on its tip
And reached, and plucked a full professorship.

With his Ph.D. under his belt, or wherever he keeps it, the Young Instructor knows more names, dates, titles of books, and other useless facts than he will ever again know. The only thing he doesn't know is how to teach. How he keeps the students from knowing this is a professional secret, and how the students keep from letting him know they know is truly remarkable. When the Young Instructor is asked something he is hazy about, he immediately comes back with, "What do *you* think?" This not only flatters the student but may provide the Young Instructor with an answer he can use next time. Anyhow, it is better than losing face, when you are down to the last one.

Well, here he is. Few but his closest friends and all the people they have told know that he is considering giving up teaching at the end of the year and going into business with his father:

Young Instructor

Crammed tight with knowledge still to be digested,
Quick-triggered with some quite impressive quotes,
Completely competent, they say, and tested
In use of bibliography and notes,
He joins a large department, at the bottom,
Not yet in campus politics entwined,
And teaches, with the turn of leaves in autumn,
The courses those promoted left behind.
To freshman, row on row and greenly glistening,
He tenders information as he's hired to,
And they, in turn, between their yawns are listening
For one persuasive reason: they're required to.

Before you feel too sorry for this next person, the Graduate Assistant, remember that he doesn't *have* to teach and study simultaneously. He could study full time if he were willing to borrow a few thousand dollars and have this debt hanging over him for the next ten years. The following portrayal does not apply to the Graduate Assistant in Physics or Engineering, whose only problem is deciding between the subsidies offered him by government and by business:

Graduate Assistant

Like Chaucer's Clerk of Oxenford,
    He has a hollow look,

And in his head is freshly stored
  The contents of a book.

Gladly would he learn, if he
  Could give full time to studying,
But till he gets his Ph.D.
  His bloodshot eyes keep bloodying

From reading students' papers through
  (His reddened eyes are misting)
To save the time (and eyesight, too)
  Of him he is assisting.

And gladly would he teach. He sees
  Himself a scholar-leader,
A full professor, if you please,
  With, best of all, a reader.

But till his dissertation's done
  And someone says he passes,
He'd best live sparely, limit fun,
  And buy some stronger glasses.

And now, as we quietly approach the Delivery Desk,
which is not what it seems to be, this being a college
library and not a hospital, we come upon one of the
most curious species of academic fauna:

Librarian

Behind the desk, behind the shelf,
She seems the shyest sort of elf,
Or, mingled in with cabinets

And catalogues and books in sets
And paste and shears and rubber bands,
A small machine with human hands.
Her tread is light as down or feather.
Her shoes can hardly be of leather.
She speaks a muted sort of speech;
Her words, half whispered, barely reach.
But out of hours, who knows? Perhaps
She stamps her feet and shouts and claps

Librarian

Her hands and goes on quite a buzz—
At least, one rather hopes she does.

Persons who supply money for private colleges are known as donors, while those who supply money for state institutions are known as taxpayers. Donors are harder to deal with, because they cannot simply be billed, nor can they be jailed if they fail to pay. That is why the private college's Director of Development is so envious of his opposite number, the Tax Collector. More has been written about, and to, the Tax Collector than the Director of Development. Hence, to even things up a little, the following lines:

Director of Development

A single-minded chap, his task
Is but to ask and ask and ask,
To split a man and wealth asunder,
To cultivate—but not plow under.
He spends his time among the rich
(When in their midst, his fingers itch),
And on his slide rule deftly he
Works out their life expectancy.
He hopes they're not too much encumbered
And that at least their heirs are numbered.

His walls are hung with plans and drawings
Of buildings that bring ohs and ahings
And promises, a trifle rash,
And sometimes small amounts of cash.

His talk is full of pressing needs,
Annuities, and trusts and deeds
And salaries and new construction
And how to get a tax deduction.
His suit is neat and rather fine;
His tie clasp is a dollar sign.

Just as the Director of Development tries to get money for the college, the Placement Director tries to get money for the college graduate. Sometimes he is almost too successful:

Placement Director

Who weeps not for the placement lad
    Must have a heart of stone.
He gets jobs for the college grad
    That pay more than his own.

Since publication of Polly Adler's *A House Is Not a Home,* I have been embarrassed to refer to a House Mother as a House Mother. But Home Mother doesn't seem quite right either. Anyhow, she means well:

House Mother

She mothers her chicks like a mother hen
And lays an egg
Now and then.

One way to get an examination or a term paper postponed is to obtain a written excuse from the College Physician. Sometimes a student who is not sick can wangle this precious piece of paper, especially a major in Drama, who can look desperately ill when well. But the College Physician usually sees through such things, via the nose and mouth:

College Physician

M.D. among the Ph.D.s,
This doctor doctors, if you please.
At games he sits upon the bench
Beside the Coach and notes each wrench
That sprains an ankle, twists a back—
And calms the Coach, who cries, "Alack!"
But mostly he's involved, I'm told,
In coping with the common cold,
The cough, the sneeze, the runny nose,
In countless Janes and countless Joes.
Half jestingly he says, in fact,
His home is in the Bronchial Tract.
So narrow is the range of ills
On which he works with shots and pills,
He sometimes dreams about theatrics
Of strokes and such in geriatrics,
Or racing on a sudden mission
As does the summoned obstetrician.
But then, he pays no office rent,
Indeed he isn't out a cent
For overhead or bills unpaid,
And that is why these years he's stayed
And why he'll stay, thus guaranteed,
And very slowly go to seed.

The college is constantly in search of good publicity, and constantly terrified at the thought of bad publicity. Somewhere out there, beyond the college walls, is the Public, just ready to pounce. The touchiest part of the Public is the Local Community, which resents all the college's tax-free property and thinks more members of the faculty should belong to the American Legion. The Local Community, which is rather humorless, is unable to see anything funny about such student pranks as putting flour in the air conditioner at City Hall and painting obscene words on the south wall of the County Library. The Director of Public Relations, not helped any too much by student picketing and riots, tries his best, but keeps mumbling about having been a fool to leave his job as crime reporter with a Midwestern daily:

Director of Public Relations

The name of the college he spreads far and wide.
Has somebody done something—published or died?
Has a faculty member addressed the Kiwanis?
Is Founder's Day, Campus Day, some Day upon
    us?
Did a speaker speak up at a student assembly
And make some remarks that left everyone trembly,
And must it be shown that, despite what some
    think,
Every speaker is neither Red nor a Pink?

In his left hand a phone, in his right hand some
    copy,

Behind him machines going "cloppety-cloppy,"
He stares at his walls, white as new-fallen snow
With clippings—the ones he is willing to show.
Deploring what didn't get printed but should
And also what did, and that did us no good,
He busies himself with the press, you can see,
And no one's so pressed or depressed as is he.

The Dietitian is between Scylla and Charybdis. The
students want steak three times a day, but the President
says, "Stay within your budget," which means casse-
roles. One problem of the Dietitian is how to serve a
casserole that will look and taste like a New York cut.
She does her best:

Dietitian

She learned some years ago (she's clever)
    What since has kept her from defeat,
And this is what she learned: you never
    Ask students what they want to eat.

She knows of carbohydrates, starches,
    Buys by the case and by the gross,
Could use leftover linnets' arches,
    She figures everything so close.

Her first concern, as dietitian,
    Is cutting costs (nine eggs serve ten).
Her second is, of course, nutrition.
    Her third is cutting costs again.

One man who starts at the ground floor and works up is the Custodian. Sometimes, however, to vary the routine, he starts at the top floor and works down. He doesn't want to get into a rut, like the professors. Working around a college, he should pick up an education, along with everything else he picks up and carries off to the trash pile. His office is where you go for Lost and Found articles. Sometimes he is pretty hard to find himself, especially when he is desperately needed to cope with an emergency which is beyond faculty skills, such as a burnt-out fuse or a stuck toilet. Usually, though, he stays close to his office, where he has a radio, a Thermos of coffee, and stacks of old magazines he has fished out of professors' wastebaskets, some of which would surprise you. To sum up:

Custodian

The man they used to call a Janitor
Ranks well above a U.S. Sanitor
Around a college, for I doubt
That you could get along without
This chap with mop and broom and rag
Who scrapes up gum and hoists the flag
And finds the notebooks, pens, and pencils,
The grade books, folders, maps, and stencils
That learned people, short of mind
But long on knowledge, leave behind.
He's known upon a first-name basis
And he, in turn, knows names and faces

Of students, faculty, alums
More than their colleagues or their chums.
And loyalty? He's quite fanatical.
He should have tenure and sabbatical.

Commencement is one time when the outside world, not being privileged to attend faculty meetings, gets to see all the members of the faculty together. Faculty attendance at Commencement is good not only because it is required but because the average professor, who looks below average in a business suit, looks really impressive in a cap and gown and doctoral hood, and knows it. Professors would look even more impressive if the hood were worn over their heads, as it was in the days of the Spanish Inquisition and still is at meetings of the Ku Klux Klan. It's quite a sight, all these learned scholars walking along, in strict order of seniority, now and then doing a double shuffle as they try to get back in step:

Academic Procession

Untended and unplucked, unstrewn,
Unornamental, June to June,
Professors, in their special way,
Are plants that bloom a single day.

Burst suddenly in blazing flower,
They for a brief exciting hour
Enchant and awe the lookers on
Who witness the phenomenon.

And then, as suddenly, they shed
Their brilliant petals, go quite dead,
And stay inexplicably sere
Until Commencement comes next year.

Commencement is also when a strange phenomenon,
called a Reunion, occurs. This is when graduates com-
pulsively and irrationally return to the college, like
lemmings. One such occasion is this:

Twenty-Fifth Reunion

Well, here we are, with husbands and with wives,
Accounting for the passage of our lives,
Remembering the good old good old days
And singing good old Alma Mater's praise
And smiling and exchanging commonplaces
While trying hard to bracket names and faces.
New, unfamiliar buildings frame the Quad,
But these are not so startling, not so odd
As what abrasive years have done to hair
And teeth and such. Oh no, we mustn't stare,
We mustn't start, or grow the slightest teary
But only slap the stooping back and query,
"How many children have you?" "What's your
    line?"
And always comment on the answer, "Fine!"
The bald wear hats, the ones with dentures hold
Their lips a trifle tight, the fat ones fold
The flesh in so that it will be the least apparent....
Be kind, we tell ourselves, and be forbearant,

And afterward let not a moment pass:
Go home and look into the looking glass.

Let us leave them there, each marvelling at how much the other has changed and, if they see any of their old professors, marvelling that these worthies are still alive.

XV

HOW TO BURN A BOOK

Nothing causes so much trouble around a college as books. Professors have to write them to get promoted. Students have to read them to stay in college. Trustees have to raise money to build libraries to house them. No wonder there is so much interest today in reducing the number of books by burning them—on a selective basis, of course.

Book burning is a charming old custom, hallowed by antiquity. It has been practiced for centuries by Fascists, Communists, atheists, school children, rival authors, and tired librarians. Like everything of importance since the invention of the cloak and the shroud, its origins are cloaked in mystery and shrouded in secrecy. Some scholars believe that the first instance of book burning occurred in the Middle Ages, when a monk was trying to illuminate a manuscript. All agree that book burning was almost non-existent during the period when books were made of stone. With the coming of papyrus, book burning made a long stride forward.

One of the most famous literary references to book burning occurs in Shakespeare. In *The Tempest* (Act

A charming old custom

III, scene ii), Caliban gives the following helpful advice to his fellow conspirators when they are plotting to overcome Prospero:

> Why, as I told thee, 'tis a custom with him
> I' th' afternoon to sleep. There thou mayst brain
>   him,
> Having first seized his books; or with a log
> Batter his skull, or paunch him with a stake,
> Or cut his wezand with thy knife. Remember
> First to possess his books; for without them
> He's but a sot, as I am, nor hath not
> One spirit to command: they all do hate him
> As rootedly as I. Burn but his books.

Since this custom is so ancient and has been practiced so continuously, it might seem strange that there is need at this time for instruction regarding how to burn a book. The need, however, is not only real but urgent. Many of those currently engaged in book burning are not themselves readers or possessors of books, and thus are unable to cope effectively with the destruction of these unfamiliar objects. For those who are able to read, it is hoped that these instructions will be found helpful.

Unless the fire has already been brought to an extremely high temperature, it is not advisable to burn a book whole. The first step is to remove the binding, which is the outer part and has very little printing on it. If this should happen to be buckram or leather, it may be necessary to pour gasoline upon it to increase its flammability. (These instructions may be ignored if the book—as there is an increasingly good chance will be the case—has a paper binding. Moreover, the book burner may wish to spare such bindings out of deference for the women who are depicted upon them.)

Once the binding is removed, the book's pages should be taken out a few at a time. If the pages have been cunningly stitched together, instead of glued, this may be a laborious process, but one well worth the effort. Fifty or a hundred pages fastened together will be found to burn with exasperating slowness, and the expenditure of a considerable amount of gasoline may be required. On the other hand, five or ten pages will burn quite rapidly. Although it may take a little more time at first, removal of the pages one by one will pay off in the end. Each individual page will burn quickly, give off a lovely flame, and leave almost no ash. The page-by-page method of book burning is strongly recommended.

Where to burn books is a matter of individual preference. Some experienced book burners report that they use an ordinary fireplace or backyard incinerator with good effect. Although less efficient than wood, coal, or peat, books make a bright flame and will warm a small room if the fire is fed continuously. Except for books bound in morocco and calf, they do not leave clinkers. For cooking, and especially for use in the barbecue pit, books are of convenient size but have certain serious drawbacks. They give off an unsteady heat and lack the lingering glow of charcoal. In an emergency, however, they will serve the purpose.

An increasingly popular place for book burning is the middle of a street or, even better, a town square. This makes possible the burning of a larger number of books at one time, and the fire may become intense enough for the burning of whole books, thus eliminating the necessity of the painstaking separation of pages referred to above. Another advantage is that this type of burning can be watched by a large number of townspeople and can become something of a social event. Community sings often develop spontaneously on such occasions, and many persons stay late to reminisce about other book burnings and to tell stories by the waning fire. It is well to watch the direction of the wind, and to have fire apparatus nearby in case the blaze should get out of hand. It is also foresighted to engage additional street cleaners to sweep up the ashes and partially burnt bindings the next day. Some towns have returned a handsome profit by selling the concession for refreshments, souvenirs, and other items likely to be desired by the crowd of onlookers.

Since the invention of printing, book burning has lagged seriously behind book production. Suggestions have recently been offered from all sides, especially the left side and the right side, about how to close this dangerous gap. Burning the individual book is slow and toilsome, and many scores and even hundreds of copies of a book may be produced while half a dozen copies are

being burned. One proposal, under serious consideration in some quarters, is to burn libraries instead of
books. Another plan envisages burning publishing
houses.

In this brief treatment of the subject, there is no
space to discuss in detail the merits of these various
proposals. The burning of individual books has an element of sport in it, and permits a considerable amount
of what is known as audience participation. The burning of libraries is a large-scale, practical solution to the
problem, and the resulting conflagrations would, it is
admitted, be spectacular. The burning of publishing
houses is an admirable idea, although since most publishing houses are in New York City, persons in other
parts of the country would have to be content with
watching the blazes over television.

The simplest and most efficient method, and one
that would afford a great deal of pleasure to a large
number of persons, seems to us to have been overlooked
by the specialists in this field. It would get even closer
to the source, would be nation-wide, and would be
without hazards or ill effects. It is so obvious that we
wonder it has not gained general acceptance long before this. *Why not burn authors?* We are confident that,
now that this has been proposed, the delightful simplic-
ity of the method will be apparent to everyone. Author-
burning is likely to become widespread, and it is hoped
that the authors themselves will enter in wholeheartedly.
It may be the greatest thing since Gutenberg.

Why not authors?

ABOUT THE AUTHOR

Richard Armour, though writing playfully and irreverently, is thoroughly familiar with the academic scene. A graduate of Pomona College and a Ph.D. from Harvard, he has been most of the things he writes about: undergraduate, graduate student, instructor, assistant professor, associate professor, professor, visiting professor, and dean of the faculty. He has taught for thirty-seven years in a wide variety of institutions, including small colleges, large universities, coeducational institutions, colleges for women, and a graduate school. In addition he has held research fellowships in England and France, was American Lecturer at the University of Freiburg in Germany, and has lectured at scores of colleges and universities throughout the United States. At present Balch Lecturer in English Literature at Scripps College in Claremont, California, he bases his "low view of higher education" on no one institution—least of all the institution with which he is currently connected. Rather, he draws upon his knowledge of many campuses, as well as his not inconsiderable imagination.

Though he is best known for his shrewd spoofs of history and literature, such as *It All Started with Columbus, Twisted Tales from Shakespeare,* and *American Lit Relit,* Richard Armour started his career as a serious scholar. He wrote impressive volumes of biography and literary criticism until he became a full professor with tenure and found this sort of thing no longer necessary. Light and serious, verse and prose, this is his twenty-ninth book.

ABOUT THE ARTIST

Tennessee-born Leo Hershfield, illustrator of innumerable books and articles, has traveled far and wide (he has just returned from Nigeria, as a matter of fact, on an assignment for the State Department). His travels have covered New York City (where he studied at the Art Students League and worked for *The New York Times* and other papers), Washington (where he sketched Senate filibusters), Dallas (where he portrayed the Ruby trial), and various sketching tours for television. He lives in Florida, where he has time for such hobbies as sailing, painting watercolors, and reading Richard Armour, this being the sixth of his books he has illustrated.